2,50

Practical Business Genius

Practical Business Genius

&

50 Smart Questions Successful Businesspeople Ask

Craig R. Hickman

John Wiley & Sons, Inc.

New York • Chichester • Brisbane • Toronto • Singapore

Library of Congress Cataloging-in-Publication Data

Hickman, Craig R.
    Practical business genius : 50 smart questions successful
businesspeople ask / by Craig Hickman.
        p.   cm.
    Includes bibliographical references.
    ISBN 0-471-53206-1 (acid-free paper)
    1. Industrial management.   I. Title.
HD31.H48156   1991
658.4—dc20   91-15688

Printed in the United States of America.
10 9 8 7 6 5 4 3 2 1

To the people who helped me ask
the right questions and find the right
answers for this book:

MICHAEL SNELL
MARCELLO HUNTER
JOHN MAHANEY
MARY KOWALCZYK
DIL KULKARNI
LES FORSLUND
ERIC MARCHANT
CARL BACON
JIM MCDONALD
JOE CANNON
REID ROBISON
STAN VARNER
PAM HICKMAN

Preface

--- ❧ ---

*The wise man doesn't give the right answers,
he poses the right questions.*

Claude Lévi-Strauss

*F*or most of us, it gets harder to rise above the day-to-day chaos of contemporary corporate life and find the time to ask the right questions, much less to answer them. So many distractions tug at our attention in this war-torn, recession-drained, competition-rabid, downsized world that whether we're CEOs, senior executives, division presidents, department heads, first-line supervisors, or filling some other assignment in the organization, we spend most of our time putting out fires, writing reports, resolving conflicts, making presentations, defending our positions, and treating symptoms of problems. We desperately need to relax, step back from the fray, and think long and hard about the really vital questions upon which our long-term success depends.

Specifically designed to give you those sorely needed hours or minutes during which you can strike at the heart of your business, asking and answering the vital questions, *Practical Business Genius: 50 Smart Questions Successful Businesspeople Ask* poses and helps answer the toughest questions facing any organization today. Whether you're dealing with strategic issues of global positioning and foreign competition, corporate culture demands involving employee commitment and empowerment, mounting pressure for changes resulting from customer complaints and competitor advancements, or frustrating obstacles to productivity, effectiveness, and bottom-line results that mercilessly cast short-term roadblocks on the path to long-term success, you can use this book to gain the right perspective when planning, investing, evaluating, and improving.

Years of research into what makes companies tick, hundreds of consulting projects, and endless discussions with thousands of business men and women around the world have convinced me that ten transcendent issues lie at the core of every business: *Customers, Quality, Service, Advantage, Talent, Motivation, Trust, Technology, Alliances,* and *Costs.* The way in which individuals and teams deal with these ten issues largely determines their organizations' success or failure in the five key performance areas of *Strategy, Culture, Change, Effectiveness,* and *Results.*

This book examines each of the ten business issues within the context of the five performance areas through 50 penetrating questions that every individual, team, and organization must ask to survive and thrive in the 1990s. You can think about and apply the 50 questions any way you want, using the whole agenda or certain parts of it in a highly structured setting, such as a formal retreat or strategy session, or simply browsing through various questions on a quiet evening or long weekend away from the office. However you decide to use this book, front to back or back to front or even sideways, you'll eventually want to put all 50 questions together, leaving no corner of your company, division, department, function, or team unexamined.

If the 1980s urged us to ask the "right questions," the 1990s are forcing us to come up with better "right answers." As you proceed through the following questions, you'll see how others have tried to answer them. Those answers may or may not work for you, but they should, in any event, get you thinking about and dealing with the really vital issues facing your organization.

Before beginning, you may want to spend a few minutes reviewing the table of contents and the Acid Test grid at the end of the book to help you decide where to start and how to continue.

Contents

Contents

Contents

Practical Business Genius

Part I

CUSTOMERS

1

What Customer Needs Are You Trying to Satisfy?

&

A door-to-door salesman showed up on my doorstep one Saturday afternoon not too long ago and immediately started trying to sell me a new solvent he claimed would clean anything and everything. When I told him I wasn't interested, he pulled a couple of prints from a large portfolio bag and asked if I was interested in buying any original art by local artists. When I told him I wasn't interested in that, either, he proceeded to hand me a brochure describing a set of children's books guaranteed to boost my children's grades in school. No sale. But that didn't stop the enterprising fellow, who proceeded to offer a variety of services from lawn care to window washing. By this time, I was very amused with this young man and asked him how he came upon his unique approach to selling. He smiled, "Everybody needs something, so I just keep pitching until I find out what they really need or until they tell me to get lost." As it turned out, I ended up paying this young man to wash the windows on my house. His approach, it turned out, could be quite effective, and strangely, it reminded me of recent changes at an old, steadfast American company.

Procter & Gamble, always keen to retain its reputation as a savvy marketer, has been trying a lot of new approaches lately. The old mass-marketing approach that involved taking a single product to a large market through national advertising has gone the way of the dinosaur because it cannot accommodate increasingly diversified consumer needs. To fill the multitude of new customer pockets, niches, and segments requiring different kinds of products, services, and messages, Procter & Gamble has instigated micro-marketing.

How does it work? Take a product as simple as Crest toothpaste. Today, Procter & Gamble markets that single product with numerous distinct advertising campaigns directed at different markets, each with its own preferences or set of buying habits, and the company packages the product in a variety of different ways to appeal to the needs of each of those segments. Crest must appeal to the "kids" market, the "white teeth" market, the "no cavities" market, the "dentist approved" market, the "gum disease" market, the "tastes good" market, and the "fresh breath" market, and that's not possible anymore with just one kind of Crest toothpaste and one approach to marketing. Today, the company must analyze more variables than ever before in order to come up with the right advertising campaign, the right promotion, the right kind of discounts, the ideal labeling and packaging, and even the right sorts of contests, parties, and activities that can motivate a particular customer segment. The data available to Procter & Gamble and other consumer product marketers from checkout scanners boggles the mind. With the new technology, companies can get immediate data on what's working and what's not.

What Procter & Gamble does today makes what it did a few short years ago look prehistoric. Instead of one TV commercial to promote a product or group of products, Procter & Gamble creates six to ten commercials directed at different market segments and designed to air on different networks, cable channels and video programs. It conducts point-of-purchase radio advertising. It advertises on videocassettes and on wallboards in high schools and dentists' offices. It organizes local promotions and sponsors local events such as the "Pepto Bismol Chili Cooking Contest," the

"Sing in the Shower Coast Soap Contest," and a host of beauty contests, block parties, and carnivals. And even as the new micro-marketing comes into full swing, Procter & Gamble continues experimenting. What's all this doing to the products that Procter & Gamble manufactures? For one thing, it spurs the creation of a wider variety of distinct products, and as different product varieties, sizes, packages, and forms continue to proliferate at Procter & Gamble, so will its need to extend its micro-marketing approach.

❧ The Key Question

Are you fully aware of your customers' precise needs and of your organization's success in satisfying those needs?

Procter & Gamble's Answer

Procter & Gamble continues toying with a lot of different marketing approaches to see what works and what doesn't. With a huge bag of tricks at its disposal, it can spread the risk of marketing decisions across a whole host of activities, knowing that at least some will provide incremental benefits. Procter & Gamble's micro-marketing may strike you as a shotgun approach to satisfying customer needs, but if you think about it, you'll come to appreciate how it allows the company to quickly adjust the sights of its rifle as it keeps blasting away at the moving targets. The data gained from a number of promotions and campaigns across numerous segments help the company fine-tune marketing efforts and zero in on the bull's-eyes.

Suggested Right Answers

Before you launch any kind of customer satisfaction program, you should consider the following guidelines:

1. *Think constantly about your customers' specific needs.*

2. *Be realistic about which customer needs you can satisfy and which you can't.*

3. *Remain flexible and creative. Changing customer needs require innovative approaches.*

4. *With both old and new campaigns, steadily monitor the degree to which you really do satisfy your customers.*

Applying Right Answers

Everyone at a medium-sized industrial equipment manufacturing firm claimed that he or she understood the exact needs of the firm's customers. However, a newly hired marketing analyst (I'll call her Susan) who felt she had spotted some important changes in the needs of the company's target customers, could not get anyone else to agree. In Susan's view, while the company had been a market leader in warehouse and materials-handling equipment over the years, it was not paying attention to an increasing trend toward decentralization and downsizing of facilities among its customers, which added up to a growing need for lighter weight, smaller, less expensive equipment. Customers moving to smaller multiple warehouse locations clearly did not require the same kind of equipment they had used with their larger single warehouses. In addition, because fewer people staffed the smaller warehouses, a need had arisen for everyone to get suitable training on how to safely operate different types of equipment. To Susan, this indicated a rapidly growing need for smaller, easier-to-operate equipment.

To convince senior management of her thinking, Susan prepared a detailed analysis in which she specifically demonstrated that the needs of customers had shifted in recent years and that the company would lose market share if it did not shift toward less expensive, simpler-to-use equipment. Although senior management applauded Susan's analysis, no one felt any sense of urgency and therefore chose to continue to watch the trends over the next few years before making any changes. Susan strenuously objected, citing her quantitative review of competitors' products, the results of a market survey, and spot field interviews with actual customers, and even projected specifications for the equipment customers had included on their long-range shopping lists. Still, she just couldn't pry senior management away from its assumption that it knew what was going on in the marketplace and could take its sweet time responding to any changes.

Not surprisingly, two competitors, one Japanese and one Korean, introduced a number of new and modified products over the next two years that came quite close to Susan's specifications. These alternatives took a devastating chunk out of her company's market share. Recalling the experience vividly, Susan recounts how one senior executive stopped her in the hall one day and said, "Susan, why didn't you make us listen when you told us we weren't paying attention to customer needs?" Susan simply looked at him in astonishment, saying, "I had a professor in business school who seemed to have gone deaf the minute he got tenure. That's quite a common disease among executives." Though shocked by her bluntness, that executive championed Susan's promotion to Director of Marketing, a position in which she could help the company regain its "hearing."

2

Do You Make Customer Satisfaction a Total Concern?

≥∢

Lots of companies claim to make customer satisfaction a total concern, but few really do it. My Macintosh computer was under warranty for a year after I purchased it, but when the warranty ran out, I neglected to purchase the "Apple Care" program for continued service protection. Well, wouldn't you know it, my hard drive crashed, and I couldn't access my files or programs. Feeling distraught and angry, I took my computer down to the local Apple Service Center where the service manager said, "Umm, this looks bad." After running a few tests on the computer, he concluded that I would have to purchase a new hard drive, for about $800. If my computer had still been under the initial warranty protection, or if I had been an Apple Care customer, he would have happily replaced the hard drive for free. Since the Apple Care program only costs about $200 per year, my neglect was going to cost me $600. Fortunately, the service manager understood the need for satisfied customers and said he would take a look at my hard drive that evening to see what he could do to salvage it. I was elated the next morning when he called and said, "It's fixed." I immediately drove down to the Service Center, picked up my machine and signed up for the Apple Care program. By the way, he charged me only $35 for fixing my hard drive.

You don't have to be in a modern high-tech business to make customer satisfaction a constant concern. Railroads were among the first businesses to incorporate many of the scientific management practices that launched the era of modern management in the late 1800s. Over time, however, those companies naturally evolved through the life-cycle stages of emergence, growth, maturity, and decline. During the maturing and declining stages, the railroad companies lost touch with their external worlds when they turned their attention almost exclusively inward. Union Pacific is a good example. In its maturing years, Union Pacific paid for its inattention to shippers' needs by watching helplessly as the trucking industry poached on its once private domain. Instead of taking stock of its situation and waking up to the realities of customers' shipping needs, Union Pacific became more and more concerned with its own internal agendas. No one in the organization worried about whether customers' goods arrived on time, whether customers received accurate bills, whether or not faulty boxcars jeopardized customers' goods, or whether a new system might be needed for tracing misdirected shipments. Union Pacific's bureaucratic and unresponsive organization had allowed departments such as marketing, engineering, and operations to become separate kingdoms that set their own self-serving policies and rarely coordinated with other functions. Meeting budgets meant so much more to the bureaucrats than meeting customers' needs that they would even cancel cargo pick-ups or reduce the number of locomotives on a line in order to achieve predetermined budget goals. Amazingly, all of this was still going on in the 1980s, long after "close-to-the-customer" had become an honored cliché in most industries.

Railroads may have been the first to embrace modern management practices a century ago, but now companies like Union Pacific Railroad are struggling with the most rudimentary concepts of customer service and satisfaction.

❧ The Key Question

How do you create and maintain an organizational culture that concentrates on satisfying customers' needs?

Union Pacific's Answer

A few years ago, Union Pacific Corp., the parent company of Union Pacific Railroad, brought Mike Walsh in from Cummins Engine to run the railroad company. A man of action, Walsh instinctively knew how to create a customer-oriented new culture, but first he had to convince his managers to stop worrying about internal concerns and cast their gazes outward. To gain the commitment of the railroad company's management ranks, without which he never could have transformed the culture, Walsh streamlined six layers of management, pushed power and authority way down in the organization, removed barriers between departments, encouraged managers to do whatever it took to solve problems, listened to employees, and invested in a state-of-the-art computerized train-dispatching facility that could track every shipping variable. Walsh didn't agonize over all these changes, he just did what seemed necessary to get a behemoth culture to start looking beyond its own insulated world.

Has Walsh really transformed Union Pacific's culture? The full answer to that question will not come for a few more years, but to date, progress does seem promising. Locomotive availability, billing accuracy, and customer satisfaction ratings have all increased, and surveys of customers show that Union Pacific has moved from last place to first place among railroad companies. Profits experienced healthy increases in 1988, 1989, and 1990, return on assets rose from 5 percent to almost 7 percent, and, on some routes, the company recaptured as much as 15 percent of the freight market from truckers. So what's been the biggest difference at Union Pacific since Walsh climbed aboard? Many more people in the company regularly ask customers how UP can serve them best—the question has become a cultural norm.

Suggested Right Answers

Over the years, I've compiled these ten prescriptions for creating and maintaining customer-oriented cultures:

1. *Develop a gut feel for the "customer" and the customer's needs, no matter what your specific job.*

2. *Include information about satisfying customers' needs every time you consider or discuss business issues.*

3. *Plan strategically, operationally, functionally, and financially to better satisfy current and future customer needs more fully.*

4. *Make sure any statement or campaign promoting corporate values includes values dealing with customer satisfaction.*

5. *Evaluate all organizational performance in terms of satisfying customer needs.*

6. *Praise, recognize, and celebrate people for effectively meeting customers' needs.*

7. *Organize and reorganize work and structures to better satisfy customer needs.*

8. *Develop and redevelop systems and processes to deliver continuously improving customer satisfaction.*

9. *Train and retrain people to find better and better ways to satisfy the customer.*

10. *Never let any part of the organization stop looking for better ways to satisfy customer needs.*

Applying Right Answers

Two years had gone by since the shop foreman (I'll call him Ray) had retired from a 30-year career with a medium-sized, although internationally recognized, drill bit manufacturer. Now, the president of the company was asking him to consider coming back once a week for the next six months or so to provide training and guidance to individuals on the shop floor. The request hardly surprised Ray, who knew from his buddies still at the plant that things were not going well for the new shop foreman, the second one since Ray's retirement. Both foremen had been bombarded with customer complaints that the quality of drilling bits had deteriorated in Ray's absence. Flattered by the president's invitation, Ray agreed to come into the office for one day a week for a month.

Ray called a day ahead to arrange a meeting with the latest shop foreman (I'll call him Bart). Even over the phone, Ray could sense Bart's reluctance, so he tried to soften his return to the scene by simply telling Bart that he missed his old job and just wanted to talk over old times.

When Ray and Bart go together, Ray casually asked Bart when he had last sat down with people in the sales department to find out what kind of feedback they were getting from customers. After shooting Ray a puzzled look, Bart said, "Well, the sales manager came to me once, just to complain. Hey, I'm not a saleman, I stick to the shop floor." Ray smiled as he sat back in his chair. "That's what I thought at first, too. Actually, those flashy, fast-talking salesmen made me nervous until I got to know Joe (one of the company's senior salemen). Nice guy. Sets the pace down there. And you know, I learned more about making great drill bits from Joe over the years than I did running the shop floor."

Ray suggested that the three of them get together informally after work. To Ray's great pleasure, Joe and Bart hit it off and were soon laughing and sharing anecdotes about their jobs. At one point, Joe slapped Bart on the back, saying, "You know, I learned more about selling drill bits from Ray here than I did from years on the road." Of course, Joe couldn't manufacture a good diamond drill bit if he wanted to, but he learned from Ray some important details about the performance of different types of bits, which he could pass on to customers.

A week later, Bart ventured his own theory about turning around the customer satisfaction problems. "I guess I am a company saleman, after all. I'm not only going to get together with Joe every week on the golf course, I'm going to visit a few customers with him. Hey, I've even bought a new sport coat and tie!"

As it turned out, Ray continued to come in for the next two weeks, but Bart had taken his advice to heart and had begun applying his new-found insight with a vengeance. Almost overnight, noticeable improvements began occurring in terms of customer satisfaction, with complaints falling and compliments rising. Ray resumed his retirement and didn't come back to the company except for parties that occurred once or twice a year. Bart went on to become a vital part of the company's operation, even rivaling Ray's reputation.

3

Do You Carefully Track Changing Customer Needs?

ᔧᕉ

My teenage son had long been fascinated with fantasy and science fiction books. While on a business trip, I was browsing through a bookstore, and I found a book that I thought he would really enjoy. When I got home, I gave it to him, and he seemed pleased, but I could tell that somehow the gift didn't excite him as much as I had hoped. I felt disappointed but didn't say anything. A day or two later, I asked him about it, probing to see if somehow I had missed the mark with the book. He said, "It's a great book, Dad, but I'm not really into that stuff anymore." Even though I knew a teenager's interests could switch overnight, I had not been paying close enough attention to my own son's changing interests. The same thing can happen to even the most customer-conscious company.

The Mattel Toy Company, which makes and markets the famous Barbie doll, illustrates this phenomenon. The Barbie doll had been a smash hit for two decades prior to the 1970s, when the company experienced a slump by not paying attention to what a new generation of little girls were playing and thinking. By the late 1970s, these "customers" were not interested only in fantasies involving the kitchen, living room, or bedroom, where Barbie amused herself waiting for Ken to ask her out for a date or to get married. Now they were thinking about careers as well as families. In the early 1980s, Mattel began to use focus groups to study the playing habits of girls and discovered they were "playing" with their dolls going to work. Acting on this lead, Mattel's creative directors came up with a "Working Girl Barbie," a stylish business executive. Since designers knew little girls still liked to play with fancy clothes, they supplemented Barbie's daytime suit with a flashy nighttime costume and rolled out a new "Day to Night" Barbie in the late 1980s. The changes were so successful that Mattel introduced two new "career" Barbies. In 1989, it offered a "doctor" Barbie; in 1990, a "flight time" Barbie, who was both a pilot and a flight attendant. Then, in 1991, Mattel introduced the "Birthday" Barbie, lest customers view Barbie's life as all work and no play. To be sure, little girls still play at getting married and having a family, but now they also play at juggling work, social and family life, including Barbie's husband taking care of the children while she goes off to a convention to give a speech.

❧ *The Key Question*

What's the best way to stay current with changing customer needs?

Mattel's Answer

For Mattel, the answer to keeping current with changing customer needs involved remaining constantly in touch with the customer. In the late 1970s, it became apparent that Mattel had waited too long to modify its Barbie doll image. Consequently, the company suffered a slump that, in retrospect, it could have avoided. To its credit, Mattel did respond quickly, thus turning a slump into an opportunity for further growth, rather than the beginning of the end of a successful product. Mattel's Barbie doll sales have climbed continuously in the years since. Over 50 million Barbie dolls were sold in 1990 worldwide, accounting for more than half of the $1 billion in corporate revenues. Mattel has continued holding focus groups for the last decade, using them to address changing customer needs rather than mere likes and dislikes. Changes in needs dictate changes in product. According to Mattel executives, such ongoing incremental strategic modification of a product protects the firm from potentially dangerous, drastic changes.

Suggested Right Answers

As you attempt to remain current with changing customer needs, you may want to consider the following:

1. *Get constant feedback from your customers on changes in the usage patterns of your products or services. Periodically, ask your customers whether they expect to use your product or service differently in the future.*

2. *Never assume you know how customer needs are changing until you talk to your customers. Periodically, ask your customers whether their motivations for purchasing your products or services have changed.*

3. *Identify some new change in customer needs at least annually. Keep looking until you find some need, attitude, or desire that is changing or has changed.*

4. *Remember that you don't need to be an advertising agency or a consumer goods manufacturer to conduct a focus group. Hold at least one major feedback session with customer groups annually.*

5. *Don't get so caught up in getting feedback from customers about your new product or service that you fail to perceive sometimes subtle yet powerful trends.*

6. **When you experience a slump in product or service sales, marshal the resources immediately to find out what has changed.**

7. **Keep in mind that during change, something always remains constant. Pay attention to that fact as you modify your products or services to better meet customer needs.**

Applying Right Answers

The vice president of marketing for a regionally based snack food manufacturing company (I'll call him Art) designed a "popcorn program" that involved several different varieties of flavored, packaged popcorn, sold along with the company's potato chips, pretzels, and other snacks. The popcorn snacks did very well for about three and a half years and then fell into a slump. As Art and his staff studied what was happening in the marketplace, in an attempt to find out why the product had lost favor with customers, they only came up with more questions than answers. Eventually, due to pressures within the company to increase sales and maintain profitability, Art felt forced to eliminate the popcorn line, which had fallen from about $3 million to just over $1 million in annual sales.

Immediately, Art looked to other snack foods to fill the gap. Much to his dismay, about one year later, a regional competitor introduced its own line of popcorn snacks because it saw an opportunity for them in the vacated niche. The new products' flavors were different from those of Art's company, but they were basically still the same stuff. At least, that's what Art told himself as he assumed the new rival would fail. However, the competing company had done its homework on the flavors that appealed to customers, and its new line did extremely well, with the white Cheddar flavor becoming a bona fide blockbuster. After a mere twenty-four months, the competitor claimed to be ringing up $7 million annually with its popcorn snacks. Not surprisingly, people at Art's company began to ask why he had killed their own product. Art never could provide a good answer and eventually conceded that the company would have been better off modifying the product rather than killing it off. Art learned a hard lesson: Staying attuned to customers' changing needs and desires is more easily said than done, especially when you're under pressure to produce short-term results as well as nurture the development of long-term products and services.

4

Is Your Job Tied to Customer Satisfaction?

ॐ

When we finished building a house a few years ago, we found several mortgage companies eager for our business. Assuming we should base our decision on interest rates and other details of the loan, we made a careful comparison, but with so many similarities between the different deals, we ended up weighing the personalized service we were actually receiving from each lending officer with whom we were working. In the end, we chose one company on the basis of personal service, willingness to provide information, and overall attentiveness. Unfortunately, in the years since signing the loan, we have never seen or talked to that person again, and everyone else we have dealt with at the mortgage company has not even come close to matching the initial service. In fact, we have become very disgruntled with the mortgage company over a number of issues and were not surprised recently to see the company taken over by another firm. Clearly, the jobs of few, if any, people in that organization were tied to customer satisfaction. The initial loan officer had the right idea, but it somehow got lost along the way.

Price Savers, a wholesale warehouse company with revenues of over $800 million, and with 18 stores throughout the West and Midwest, offers a striking contrast. Acquired by Pace Warehouses in January 1991, the company has become a leader in the wholesale warehouse market by providing more exceptional service and delivering higher customer satisfaction than any wholesale warehouse in the country. Price Savers has triumphed keenly in competitive markets, such as southern California, by carefully managing the range of merchandise that it offers, the brands it carries, the displays it develops, and, most importantly, the satisfaction it guarantees each and every customer. In a constant effort to expand the boundaries of excellence within this company, Price Savers has embarked on many impressive innovations. To satisfy the needs of its "members" (the Price Savers name for customers), the company listens closely to all input and makes a conscious point of addressing all concerns. Price Savers "associates" (its name for employees) are trained to resolve any customer problem, need, or issue quickly and effectively. They adhere strictly to the motto: "Do whatever it takes to satisfy member needs." Associates are encouraged to promote member trust, to provide value and service, and to stress quality products and competitive pricing. According to Tom Grimm, Price Savers's former chairman and CEO, the value of products and customer service must be visible and perceivable by the members.

◆ The Key Question

How do you tie every job in the organization to customer satisfaction?

Price Savers's Answer

At Price Savers, every associate—no matter at what level within the organization—understands that customer satisfaction is a vital part of his or her job. When hiring associates, the company looks for certain attitudes, orientations, and skills specifically applicable to customer satisfaction. After hiring someone, it carefully provides training to increase those attitudes, orientations, and skills to make sure they support customer satisfaction over time. To accomplish this, Price Savers has incorporated six key attributes and skills in every job description and in each associate's performance evaluation and bonus plan. These include honesty, friendliness, sensitivity, innovation, self-motivation, and an overall "can-do" attitude.

Even people in finance, who have little contact with customers, must manifest these attributes and develop the associated skills. For instance, when a finance person deals with a customer's credit extension request or a collection issue or a returned merchandise issue, he or she must take customer satisfaction into account, just as much as an associate on the merchandise floor. Likewise, those associates working in merchandising must remain continually sensitive to what customers want in terms of merchandise and how special one-time buys may benefit their members. Because customer satisfaction affects every job, the display of merchandise at every Price Savers store is unparalleled. As a result, Price Savers has won distinction as one of the most successful wholesale warehouse organizations in the country. Now, Price Savers can pass its excellence and effectiveness to Pace Warehouses.

Suggested Right Answers

If you want to tie the jobs and positions in your organization to customer satisfaction, you may want to consider the following:

1. *Make sure that the tasks, responsibilities, and expectations outlined in your job descriptions include a careful tie-in to customer satisfaction.*

2. *Avoid general statements about doing "whatever it takes" to meet customer needs, and get specific in the job description regarding your organization's expectations for that particular job as it relates to customer satisfaction.*

3. *When you hire people, make sure that you screen them based on their attitudes, orientations, and experiences in delivering customer satisfaction.*

4. *Train new employees carefully to make sure they understand and apply the appropriate skills and standards to ensure customer satisfaction.*

5. *Include your organization's expectations regarding customer satisfaction in the performance evaluation of every individual in the organization.*

6. *Base awards, bonuses, pay increases, and promotions on achieving customer satisfaction goals.*

7. *Counsel or release employees who do not meet customer satisfaction expectations and standards.*

Applying Right Answers

A senior vice president for one of the world's largest food manufacturing corporations (I'll call him Tom) had recently won a promotion to a group executive position with 10 divisions reporting to him. As he undertook his initial review of the status and performance of each division, he began to recognize one common problem across all the divisions: insufficient focus on the marketplace and customers. Too many people in the divisions were just not that worried about or directed by what went on in the marketplace and couldn't care less about how customer needs were changing and what the competition was doing to meet those needs. This problem manifested itself in many ways in each of the divisions, some of which had become enmeshed in internal restructuring and overmanaging, office politics, red tape, and bureaucratic nonsense, all of which caused damaging communication problems and too much unfocused rhetoric about what a division should be doing.

After a lot of evaluating and thinking, Tom concluded the divisions needed to implement two simple steps: 1) start measuring and rewarding performance in terms of customer satisfaction, and 2) increase the number of people eligible for performance-based bonuses to include all managerial and supervisory personnel within each of the divisions. As he tried to implement these steps, Tom first tied 50 percent of all bonuses to customer satisfaction criteria associated with each particular job. He then launched the new approach with each division president. While the new approach ignited some complaining and even some kicking and screaming in certain quarters, Tom eventually persuaded all of the division presidents that the new approach would streamline their organizations and make everyone more attentive to delivering what customers wanted. The new orientation took several months to implement, but eventually people in each of the divisions began to notice a profound change taking place in the focus of employees around them and throughout their divisions, with attention shifting gradually from internal and organizational intrigue to marketplace concerns. The change really bore fruit as the divisions went through their performance evaluation cycle in the early fall of the year. After the first round of performance valuations, Tom and his division presidents made some modifications in some of the criteria (for some jobs, the criteria had been too vague and generalized, and for other jobs, the criteria simply hadn't applied). The second cycle of performance evaluations were the proof of the pudding, as people now accustomed to evaluating their own effectiveness in terms of customer satisfaction had sharpened their focus and redirected their energies toward the marketplace. Office politicking, interfunctional disputes, and excessive attention to internal process and structure issues rapidly declined. Recently, Tom exclaimed, "It became a sort of self-fulfilling prophecy. Once people really understood that their futures rested with our customers, they automatically began creating happier customers."

5

Can You Consistently Get and Keep Customers?

— ❧ —

I have developed quite a deep loyalty to one overnight carrier that has regularly gone beyond the call of duty to get me out of jams. As competition in this industry has heated up and prices have come down, I have been courted by the less expensive ones, but Federal Express still gets my business. In one case, a driver met me in the J.F.K. Airport terminal minutes before my departure for Europe, even though the deadline for package pick-up had passed. Another time, a dispatcher accomplished a special weekend delivery in an area the company does not officially service on weekends. In eight years of almost weekly sending and receiving irreplaceable reports and manuscripts, not once had I ever experienced a problem with a misrouted or lost package. However, a few months ago, several edited chapters of this book were lost when my agent and editor, Michael Snell, sent them from Boston to Provo via Federal Express. Much to the dismay of both Michael and myself, the chapters had to be re-edited. Federal Express apologized profusely, but could do nothing since the delivery person had left the package, by my instruction, on the door step. After the incident, I remember thinking about the numerous variables that affect customer loyalty.

In the chemical industry, DuPont has paid a lot of attention to the variables that affect getting and keeping customers. Because DuPont makes its money by selling chemicals, plastics, oil, coal, and fibers, it has come under extreme pressure from environmental groups concerned about cleaning up the earth. Company executives, appreciating both the vulnerability and opportunity inherent in their industry, concluded that, rather than duck the issue, DuPont should become a world leader. Doing so would naturally impress customers, both attracting new ones and retaining old ones. DuPont, however, was not just out to manage its visibility with customers. Rather, it was simply demonstrating the company's deep-seated commitment to satisfying customer needs. In one instance, DuPont developed a new series of agricultural herbicides that break down faster and leave fewer chemical residues in the soil. The safer chemicals have not only tripled sales for the category over the last five years, they have won many loyal customers. DuPont has also been working to develop water-based automotive paints that anticipate stricter federal standards for such products, and company scientists have already introduced alternative cleaning products for the electronics industry that do not rely on atmosphere-harming chlorofluorocarbons (CFCs). Other so-called "green" projects are underway in the areas of refrigeration, air conditioning, blowing agents, cleaners, and aerosols. Viewing environmental concern more as an opportunity than as a vulnerability, DuPont has touched its customers in a vital and lasting way.

⅋ The Key Question

What more than you're currently doing can you do to attract and hold on to your customers?

DuPont's Answer

DuPont answered the question by addressing a major global issue. The environmental crisis matters to DuPont's customers. To their credit, DuPont executives realized that it would take more than lip service or a superficial effort to impress those customers and to keep them loyal far into the future. Some industry observers believe that DuPont will generate $8 billion in revenues from its environmental services and environmentally safe products by the year 1995. Clearly, DuPont has not only opened up new avenues of business for itself, but it has strengthened its ties to its customers by thinking "green." DuPont understands what it means to get and keep customers, and its shareholders can testify to the attendant results.

Suggested Right Answers

When considering ways of getting and keeping customers, you might take into account the following points:

1. *If you cannot consistently attract and retain customers, your enterprise will fail.*

2. *If you can find ways to meet customer needs better and more cost effectively than your competitors, your enterprise will thrive.*

3. *No matter how complex or problematic your customers' needs, never quit trying to meet those needs.*

4. *Once you can consistently attract and keep customers, then all other success variables will become easier to manage.*

5. *Factor customers into every decision you make.*

Applying Right Answers

A corporate loan officer for a major financial institution (I'll call her Joan), had built up an impressive portfolio of clients. One of these was a rapidly growing nationwide interior design firm that netted over $200 million in revenues a year. Recently, however, the firm had found itself mired in cash problems caused by its push for continuing growth. The year before, the firm had sustained a $5 million loss, and it had barely broken even the two previous years. Concerned about the situation, Joan decided to dig in and find out what was going on. Would the design firm incur more losses in the future, and, if so, what should Joan as the corporate loan officer do to protect her own company's position?

First off, Joan assembled a team of analysts and let her client know that they were going to conduct a full review of the firm. Of course, this news dismayed the design firm's executives, but they really couldn't object. Soon, Joan's team was talking to employees, suppliers, and customers, reviewing every detail of the financial affairs of the business. After two months, the team reported some disturbing practices related to how the firm priced its services, how it accounted for work done on a particular design engagement, and, generally, how the firm accounted for internal resources. It all added up to overly casual management, the sort that, unchecked, could put the design firm out of business.

With this report in hand, Joan felt she possessed a fairly accurate overall picture of the firm's current predicament. She remembered what had most impressed her when she first took the design firm on as a client, its ability to attract and retain customers by doing superb work. Even now, not one customer interviewed by Joan's team had uttered a word of dissatisfaction. In fact, many customers were trying to figure out new ways to apply the interior design firm's services to their organizations and create better environments for their own workers and customers. This customer orientation explained why the company had so quickly grown to more than $200 million in annual revenues, ranking it among the top ten interior design firms in the United States. As Joan prepared for her own boss's review of the situation, she developed a set of recommendations for helping the interior design firm resolve the management and financial control problems, which Joan defined as "quite manageable, given this company's unparalleled track record with its customers."

Her boss accepted the report, and the design firm adhered to her recommendations for two years, after which it ran up solid earnings. Joan's confidence in a company that built itself on a foundation of satisfied customers was not misplaced.

Part II
QUALITY

6

What Level of Quality Are You Really After?

—————— ❧ ——————

You've probably experienced or heard some variation of the following story. For Christmas one year, three children received a question and answer game from their grandparents that was the hit of the holidays. The game covered a broad array of areas and offered updated questions as desired to a maximum of six new sets of questions, all included in the price of the original game. The children raced through all of the questions that came with the game by New Year's Day and prepared a request for another set of questions to be sent by mid-January. To their dismay, three requests and several weeks later, the company had not yet responded. When they tried to make contact with the company via the toll-free telephone number, they found it had been disconnected. A little digging revealed that the company had, in fact, gone out of business the November before. It had produced a great game and a brilliant idea for delivering hot off the press new questions that dealt with the most current events, but the company just couldn't sustain the level of quality. And it's not alone in that predicament.

The king of catsup, H.J. Heinz, relentlessly cut cost under the supervision of CEO Anthony O'Reilly. However, O'Reilly discovered that his "to-the-bone" tactics, which included downsizing and speeded up production lines, had ultimately reduced the quality of Heinz products. Quality declines, of course, erode bottom lines in the long-term. This was not an easy lesson for the company to learn, especially in the wake of increasing profit margins year after year. Strategically, product quality had taken a back seat to increasing profit margins and cost savings, and eventually quality cried out for more attention. The predicament prompted a lot of soul searching at Heinz. As customers and distributors began to notice quality glitches, sales began to falter slightly, and when management finally woke up to the fact that quality considerations had been grossly neglected, they found they had gotten out of touch with a number of quality factors. Exactly what level of quality did the company really want to deliver? It wasn't just the quality of their products that concerned O'Reilly's executives but the quality of the production process, as well.

❧ The Key Question

How can you determine the "strategically right" level of quality?

Heinz's Answer

As Heinz managers shifted their focus from cost cutting, downsizing, and margin enhancing to quality, they discovered some surprising things—most importantly, that a focus on levels of quality sheds new light on costs. A relatively small shift toward delivering strategically identified levels of quality (i.e., levels of quality demanded by customers consistent with economic feasibility) caused Heinz to *add* workers and to *slow down* the production line. For example, the managers of the Heinz Ore-Ida potato processing plants had, until recently, taken a very hard-nosed approach to cost cutting, downsizing, streamlining, and speeding up production, but by doing so they had changed the taste and texture of that division's product, Tater Tots, which disappointed consumers and prompted a decline in sales. The high-speed production process, it turned out, diced the potatoes too finely, causing the product to become too mushy. With the new focus on quality, the managers slowed down the high-speed slicing machines. Efficiency, of course, went down, but effectiveness went up as the old Tater Tot taste came back and, with it, customers. In 1989, sales of Tater Tots increased by 9 percent, more than paying for the cost of the slowdown. Heinz discovered, not only at its Ore-Ida Division but at other divisions as well, that determining the level of quality that you want to deliver puts the horse where it belongs, before the cart. Low costs don't always create happier customers, but delighted customers can pave the way toward lower costs.

Suggested Right Answers

As you attempt to determine the level of quality to offer, bear in mind:

1. *The issue of quality levels comes before cost cutting, streamlining, margin enhancing, downsizing, or other efficiency agendas.*

2. *Determine the "strategically right" level of quality you want to deliver by examining the needs of your customers, the positions of your competitors, and the capabilities of your own company.*

3. *Once you strategically determine the level of quality you want to produce or deliver, make sure you produce or deliver that level of quality from the outset.*

Applying Right Answers

Sometimes, those who stand up for a certain level of quality become martyrs in an organization. That's what happened to the resident chemist (I'll call him Dan) for a growing lawn care company in the Midwest. Dan had been hired because his Masters thesis in Biochemistry had broken new ground in the use of pesticides and fertilizers for the care of lawns and shrubs. In his new assignment, he had helped design and develop chemical mixes appropriate for the company's rapidly expanding geographical base in the Ohio Valley. Only three years old, the company had already crested $25 million in sales.

While top management congratulated itself on the company's performance, Dan began noticing a growing number of customer complaints. Dan hadn't changed the chemical mixes for three years, except to tune them up slightly, so he assumed that something else was causing customer dissatisfaction. On his own initiative, Dan began to observe what was actually going on out in the field and, to make a long story short, he soon discovered that the pressure being placed on servicemen to make more calls per day had caused them to become sloppy in their work. When Dan confronted the vice president of operations with the facts, the VP turned a deaf ear. Frustrated, Dan went to the president of the company. Again, his concerns were waved away with a smug grin. No one listened to Dan, and some executives even hinted that he stick to the chemical side of the business and stay out of the service side.

Customer complaints continued to increase to the point where the company began to lose business to new competitors. As Dan grew even more vocal about the problem, he did nothing but earn a reputation for telling others how to do their jobs. Of course, management could not ignore steadily declining sales, however, and when it did recognize the problem, it simply increased marketing and advertising budgets as well as service quotas. Dan, convinced that more hype and increased pressure on service people would never turn things around, decided to leave the company to pursue a Ph.D. His departure, it eventually became clear, was a strategic signpost someone should have viewed with alarm.

Twelve months after Dan's exit, with sales depressingly low despite massive advertising campaigns, the lawn care company finally faced up to the real problem. The vice president of operations reduced service quotas by one-third and implemented a new standard whereby bonuses were derived from zero customer complaints. New quality of service standards also came on-line in other areas such as service estimates and follow-up inspections. Within several months, sales had risen to previous levels.

Today, Dan has completed his Ph.D. and looks back with little bitterness at his "martyrdom" at the lawn care company. "I wouldn't do it differently," he chuckles. "I still own some stock in that company."

7

Are You Delivering the Quality You Promise?

---------------------- ৯ ----------------------

Our family was getting ready to host a party in our backyard last summer, and one of my responsibilities was to make sure that the yard was in tip-top shape. The morning of the party we met outside our home with the lawn care people who had arrived to cut, trim, and weed the grounds. Although we usually used them only to cut the lawn, while we did the trimming and gardening ourselves, this time we asked them to do the full job and to do it especially well. They promised that the yard would be in perfect shape by the afternoon, so we left for a few hours to take care of some other details that needed our attention before the event. When we arrived back home about an hour and a half before the party was to begin and discovered that the trimming and the gardening had only been partially completed, we were furious and spent the next hour and a half completing the job ourselves. We were still wet from our showers when guests began arriving, and we vowed to fire the lawn care company as soon as we got the chance. The next morning when they showed up to complete their job, we told them in no uncertain terms that we did not do business with people who couldn't deliver on their promises. They were shocked. It turned out that the supervisor who had promised to provide the quality of service we wanted had left faulty instructions with other members of the crew before going off to another job. Somewhere in all the communication, the quality promise had gotten lost. It happens every day in every kind of business.

After a period of strong growth in the 1970s, discount retailer K mart suffered declining sales in the late 1980s, losing customers to such aggressive new competitors as Wal-Mart. Since 1987, K mart's chairman, Joseph E. Antonini, has been trying to lure customers back to K mart by upgrading the company's image and increasing the quality of its merchandise. To help promote the cause, he hired actress Jaclyn Smith and designer Martha Stewart to tout higher-quality products in K mart's substantial apparel and housewares areas. While advertising campaigns did entice many lost customers back into K mart stores, the retailer failed to impress them once they strolled through the doors. Returning shoppers encountered the same old dreary and depressing shopping environments, with empty boxes cluttering the aisles, and merchandise carelessly tossed in heaps. Most of all, they found some of K mart's most popular and heavily advertised items out of stock.

While Antonini's vision of an upscale image and higher-quality merchandise for K mart may have been right on track, the thousands of K mart employees and managers working in the company's 2300 outlets never got the message, or, more accurately, they never really bought the new "quality" image. Consequently, a huge gap opened between the quality K mart wanted to deliver and what customers actually got.

❧ The Key Question

Does any gap exist between what you promise your customers and what you actually deliver?

K mart's Answer

In the case of K mart, Joseph Antonini ultimately tried to close the gap by augmenting the company's internal capabilities. A new $1 billion computer system, up and running by late 1990, monitors store inventory levels and speeds up the ordering of fast-moving merchandise. This system will help make sure that no customer finds an advertised product out of stock. Antonini also launched a $1.3 billion renovation and refurbishing program to enlarge, reconfigure, and update 700 of the company's oldest stores. The renovated stores promise to provide more attractive displays, more merchandise on the shelves, and an overall look and feel of higher quality. In addition, K mart began aggressively developing specialty retailing outlets such as building suppliers, hypermarkets, and membership warehouses.

Will K mart succeed in producing and delivering the kind of quality it promises? Although it's still too early to tell, the company does seem to have taken some positive initial steps. One remaining obstacle, of course, is K mart's culture, i.e., what K mart's employees and managers really believe and feel in their hearts about all this change. Have they fully committed to a higher-quality shopping experience for customers? Or, do they still feel skeptical? Whether the K marts across the country will actually deliver higher-quality shopping experiences for customers will depend a lot on how K mart managers and employees feel about the quality of their own experiences within the company, and how thoroughly they commit themselves to making sure customers never leave K mart stores disappointed with the quality of their shopping experiences and purchases.

Suggested Right Answers

When it comes to producing or delivering the quality you promise, keep in mind a few basic points:

1. *Consciously and constantly look for gaps between what you promise and what you can deliver.*

2. *Decide right now that you will never promise more than you can actually produce and deliver.*

3. *When you decide to improve quality, make sure you improve the systems, processes, technology, capabilities, and culture that produce and deliver the quality.*

4. *Implement what quality experts have been preaching for the last decade: a continuous quality improvement philosophy in your organization.*

5. *Make sure the responsibility for quality falls on everyone's shoulders, from the entry-level clerk to the CEO.*

Applying Right Answers

After completing his first year, a Northwestern MBA student (I'll call him Don) went to work for the summer as a productivity analyst for a major food-processing company on the East Coast. Having taken his undergraduate degree in engineering, Don was intent on a career in manufacturing. The food-processing company appealed to him because it had implemented a total quality system two years previously and was looking for ways to improve the system. Working there could, presumably, broaden Don's academic study of total quality systems and programs.

As Don began his assignment to assess opportunities for further improvements in quality, he had the chance to examine every system, process, technology, and method employed by the company in one particular plant. Early in the summer, he said, "I really expect to find a lot of inconsistencies between the company's self-proclaimed quality program and what its people are actually doing to implement it." To Don's amazement, however, the people at this particular plant were clearly making extraordinary efforts to align their own actions with the quality objectives outlined in the company's overall program. They seemed fully committed to making sure that everything they produced was of the best quality, that the number of rejects in canned and packaged products stayed as close to zero as possible, and that their every action led to achieving those goals.

As Don attended weekly reporting sessions with different production teams, he began to see how every topic for discussion tied into quality production in some way or another. Issues of productivity and cost control always came up in the context of product and production process quality.

As the summer progressed, Don walked through every step of the plant's production process, alert for ways to improve quality. He looked at the many inputs and outputs at every stage, determining how people did their jobs, how production systems functioned and how people responded to the challenge to improve quality while maintaining and increasing profit margins. At the end of the summer, Don submitted a report suggesting two engineering changes that could improve quality on certain processing lines without sacrificing productivity. Productivity, he had come to see, cannot function without regard to quality. The skepticism with which he had begun his assignment had evaporated, and he now believed wholeheartedly that total quality systems really can work when a sense of quality pervades the entire culture. As a result, Don returned to his second year in the Northwestern MBA program with a healthy, new, practical outlook on the value of total quality systems in organizations.

8

Do You Continuously Improve Quality?

※

Not too long ago, I was watching my daughter as she assembled a car out of a children's multicolored Lego building block set. Once she had the basic car shape together, she began sticking odd blocks on here and there, accessorizing and adding to the contraption until it no longer even looked like a car. "Sweetheart," I asked. "What are you doing?" With that exasperated sigh children reserve for thick-headed adults, she said, "I'm making it *better!*"

Now, whenever I get into a discussion with people trying to continuously improve quality, I think of my daughter's struggle to make it "better." Too often, a company's ongoing quality efforts deal too much with the frills, fooling themselves into thinking they're really improving the basics. That has not been the case, however, with the New York City subway system, which until recently epitomized urban filth and decay.

From a high of 3.1 billion passengers a year in the 1940s and 1950s, the system carried little more than 1 billion in 1983. Poorly maintained train cars, ubiquitous graffiti, filthy stations, and brutal crime had turned a once model transportation system into a dangerous joke. Was it bad management? Yes, and no. Many skilled people, whose abilities masked some of the system's flaws, had retired and been replaced by people with lesser skills, and, actually, too few managers oversaw the system's 50,000 employees. Inflexible unions, to which even supervisors belonged, called too many of the shots.

In 1983, Robert Kiley became the new chairman of the Metropolitan Transit Authority, and he named a new president, David Gunn, who had formerly taught at the Harvard Business School and who boasted a distinguished career in the Navy and a lot of experience with railroads. Determined to improve the decaying and maligned subway system, Kiley and Gunn embarked on the mammoth turnaround effort.

They overlooked no detail that contributed to the public's perception of quality, ordering all of the graffiti scrubbed from every train car on every line and making sure older cars, all of which were modernized and repaired, were treated with a graffiti-resistant paint to make them compatible with hundreds, if not thousands, of brand-new cars that would upgrade the fleet. The whole project took five years, but by 1989 the New York subway system could rightly claim that all of its 6200 cars were graffiti free. Meanwhile, behind the scenes, a continuous quality-improvement program tackled all the defective tracks, with 350 miles of new track laid by 1990 and another 550 miles planned for the future. A twice weekly inspection system insures the safety of every inch of track, and any problem is corrected within 24 hours. The number of managers had doubled, from 615 to 1200, a move aimed at giving the organization the ongoing guidance and direction it needs to keep its quality-improvement program moving ahead. Among other things, management effectiveness had weakened the union stranglehold on the system. Today, even New York's biggest detractors admit that the subway system has noticeably improved.

❧ *The Key Question*

How do you get people and organizations to strive for genuine, continuous improvement?

The New York City Subway System's Answer

For the New York City Subway System, its continuous improvement began with two experienced leaders, Robert Kiley and David Gunn. Gunn had been head of the Philadelphia system, and both men had worked together at the Boston Transit System. They felt confident that they could bring about the necessary changes in the New York system. To succeed, they knew they needed to stablize the system first, convincing everyone in the organization to stop fighting fires so that they could replace that mentality with a continuous improvement one.

In order to accomplish this stabilizing first step, Kiley and Gunn revamped priorities by undertaking basic improvements to the very essence of the system, such as tracks, tunnels, switches, and electrical systems, as well as more visible improvements, such as station remodeling, air conditioning, and other comforts. For instance, prior to the Gunn and Kiley era, unfilled parts requests ran over 25 percent, but through the constant effort to stabilize the system, they declined to under 3 percent. The Kiley-Gunn emphasis on the essential guts of the business allowed the new chiefs to shift the whole orientation of the organization to a mandate for ongoing and significant quality improvement. While many people think the subway system still has a long way to go, the second step of implementing a program of continuous improvement is well under way.

Suggested Right Answers

The guidelines below will help ensure that your own continuous improvement efforts really bring about the kind of change you seek:

1. *Commit yourself totally and completely to making changes every day that bring about continuous improvement in the core areas of your business.*

2. *Identify what really drives success in your business. Continuous quality improvement must address the very essence of your business, not just peripheral niceties or nonessentials.*

3. *Make sure everyone in your organization understands that success and rewards depend on making the core aspects of your business better.*

4. *Praise and reward improvements in the core areas of your business as highly as any other results in your organization.*

Applying Right Answers

A restauranteur (I'll call him Phil) owned and operated three eating establishments in a mid-sized Southwestern city. His newest and largest one was giving him nightmares because he couldn't figure out how to make it work. Hoping to attract college students from the local university, he had imbued the restaurant with a 1950s theme, but somehow that wasn't working. Frustrated, Phil started tinkering with the place, upgrading the decor to give it even more of a "fifties" feeling, hiring local and regional bands who played the nostalgic hits of that era, and revising the menu to give basic dishes such "fifties" sounding names as "the Eisenhower Salad" and the "Marilyn Monroe Cheesecake." Unfortunately, none of these changes brought customers dancing through the doors. After a year, Phil decided to dump the whole "fifties" theme in favor of a nautical-seafood concept. The new restaurant bore the right touches: a big neon fish over the door, aquariums in the dining room, and cute little sailor outfits for the waitresses. Three months later, however, his erstwhile customers were still sailing off to the competition.

Discouraged and depressed over two failures in a row, Phil got to chatting with an acquaintance at his local Rotary Club meeting. This woman, who ran a small chemical plant in the area, started asking some "dumb" questions about the key elements of Phil's business and ended up suggesting that Phil needed to focus on the quality of the food rather than cute costumes, themes, and menus. "You've got to get back to basics. What if I came up with fancy packaging and clever brand names for my chemicals, but put explosive mixtures in the bottles. I wouldn't even have any customers to worry about!"

At first, Phil's associate's comments offended him. What did she know about the restaurant business? Why, Phil had paid attention to the quality of the food, insisting on first class ingredients for every dish he offered. "Look," he said in exasperation, "come over to our new seafood restaurant for dinner tonight—on the house. I guarantee you'll love it."

That night when Phil greeted his friend after she had finished her dinner, she objectively pointed out that her fish had been served in a tomato sauce more befitting a hamburger than fillet of sole. The ingredients were first-class, the waitress's short skirt was painstakingly starched, the eels in the aquarium were writhing away happily, but, pointed out Phil's friend, "I wouldn't recommend the food." Phil was stunned, but he finally got the message: Get down to basics and get customers raving about the food.

A year later, Phil's Place (no fancy frills, cute costumes, or clever menus) couldn't accommodate all the customers who wanted to eat there. Word had gotten around that you couldn't beat Phil's Place for a quiet setting, excellent steaks and seafood, and impeccable service. It won four stars from the local paper and pulled in more profit than Phil's other two restaurants combined. To top it off, Phil's Rotary Club critic held her plant's annual banquet at Phil's Place, where she offered a heart-warming toast, "To the Basics!"

9

Can You Get Each Individual to Improve Quality?

❧

A major producer of electronic components had just lost one of its major accounts and had hired our firm to find out why. Management was worried because the company had lost two other major accounts over the last six months. I'll never forget interviewing an assistant manager of production. During the interview he said, "I knew we were going to lose the business because our quality has slipped." When I asked him why he hadn't said something or done something to make his feelings known earlier, he said, "Aw, nobody would listen to me." How wrong he was! When I passed his comments on to management, they immediately dove into the problem. It struck me then, as it continues to strike me, that one individual in an organization, even one far removed from customer interaction or the manufacturing plant, can make an enormous contribution to product or service quality.

In the mid-1980s, when Xerox lost such considerable market share to the Japanese, the company launched a program it called "Leadership through Quality," which would bring the company's entire strategic focus to bear on improving the quality of its products and maintaining an edge through that quality. Xerox management was intent upon more effectively adapting to the changes in the marketplace wrought by foreign competition. Xerox's quality mission statement identified the goal that Xerox become a quality company, that quality should pervade its every decision. In short, quality improvement became a central duty of every Xerox employee. In order to imbue every employee with this commitment, the company inaugurated extensive training from top to bottom. First, the company's top 25 executives went through the extensive program, then they, in turn, took the training to their immediate subordinates. The training sessions cascaded down through the company with each "teacher" passing the lessons to the next-in-command until they reached every single individual. Supplemental training took place as needed. Quality improvement and training experts were always on hand to assist the managers or supervisors as they trained their fellow workers.

᠉ The Key Question

Can you really get everyone in the organization to improve quality?

Xerox's Answer

By 1990, as Xerox engineers worked to advance copier technology, more than 100,000 employees had taken the company's 30-hour course on quality. Each person learned how the parts they produced related to all the other parts, and each gained an understanding of how the quality of his or her work related to that of workers down the line. Employees were urged to make suggestions about and contributions to quality improvements, with strong individual recognition going to those who succeeded in doing so.

Since Xerox CEO David Kearns sees training as the key to the company's future, he has made it his unrelenting passion. According to Kearns, only solid, steady training can integrate everything that goes on in an organization. Without it, no single employee or team will ever grasp a total sense of what the company is all about. This commitment to holistic training has allowed Xerox to make remarkable progress in the past few years. In fact, Xerox not only became the first American company to win back market share from the Japanese, without the benefit of tariffs or other government help, but in 1989, it won the prestigious Malcolm Baldridge National Quality Award given annually to American companies that best exemplify quality. While Xerox's market share for small copiers fell from 17 percent in 1979 to 8½ percent in 1984, it rose to 15 percent in 1990. The Malcolm Baldridge Award belonged not to a corporate entity but to the several hundred thousand individuals who made it possible.

Suggested Right Answers

As you work to make individuals in your own organization more responsible for quality improvements, you should consider the following points:

1. *Help every employee understand the importance of quality in his or her own job.*

2. *Make sure each individual appreciates how quality work in his or her position coordinates with the quality work of others throughout the entire organization.*

3. *Make sure quality is a key factor in hiring decisions, job descriptions, performance reviews, rewards, raises, and bonuses.*

4. *Train, train, train, and train some more to make sure your focus on quality improvement reaches everyone in the organization.*

5. *Listen to every individual recommendation for quality improvement. Never get caught in the trap that committees make the best decisions.*

Applying Right Answers

The manager of a chain-operated hotel in the Northeast (I'll call her Sandra) attended a three-day training program her company had designed to improve the quality of guest services. Sandra was struggling with what she had been presented because she wasn't convinced it would really work or change anything. The new program, it seemed, required every employee at every hotel in the chain to keep tabs on every other employee with whom they came in contact. This included everyone from the housekeepers to the bellhops to the information attendants and concierges. Sandra's own hotel, with 360 rooms and a staff of over 100, could, she feared, become a seething cauldron of backstabbing and finger-pointing. "I think this could be unbelievably demoralizing," she said. "The company wants quality improvement, but I'm afraid they're going to get chaos instead." However, Sandra had no choice but to give the new program a chance. As it turned out, she went back and held a series of meetings during one full week with the entire hotel staff to introduce the program, and during the program's first two weeks in operation, Sandra's worst fears came true. Where tranquility among employees had previously existed, now conflict and quarreling erupted. By the end of the second week, Sandra was convinced that this program just wasn't going to work, so she called her boss, the operations vice president, to voice her complaints. The VP of operations assured her that she was not the only one experiencing such turmoil, and that based on their research on similar programs operating in other companies, the breakthrough didn't really occur until the program had been in place for at least one month. They discussed Sandra's misgivings at length, but the VP eventually persuaded her to continue on the same course. Sandra continued.

Developments over the next two weeks surprised Sandra more than anything she had yet experienced in her business career. Amazingly, the process of keeping tabs on one another's quality turned into a very positive motivator for her staff as it actually became a game in which each employee tried harder to reach a higher standard of quality in guest services. At weekly staff meetings, jokes were made about subquality work, and stories were told about guests' gratifying reactions to the new attention to quality. The initial problems arose, it seemed, because initially people did not quite know how to handle open, ongoing critical interaction with their peers. But after a while, they came not only to feel comfortable with it but to appreciate its positive effect on their morale and the quality of their day-to-day work. Needless to say, Sandra became a staunch supporter of the new program.

10

Do You Always Deliver Above-Standard Products or Services?

❧

*T*here's an old joke about the executive who went to an exclusive tailor for a new suit. The place was so popular, the tailor was racing around frantically, trying to take a dozen customers' measurements at once. After an hour in this mayhem, the executive left with an appointment to pick up his new suit in two weeks.

When the time came, he hurried to the shop only to find the same madhouse scene, so he was surprised to find that his suit was ready. To his shock, however, one sleeve was too short, there was a noticeable hump below the back of the collar, and one pants leg was an inch too long. "No matter," said the tailor. "Just raise up one shoulder, lean to the left, bend over, reach between your legs, and pull the hem of the coat down firmly."

Edging down the street in this fashion, the executive overheard two young women discussing his condition. "Look at that poor crooked man," said one. "Yes," said the other, "but doesn't his suit fit him so nicely?"

Like that harried tailor, too many businesses let their standards slip when under pressure, hoping their customers won't notice. Of course, they always do, sooner or later.

The environmental service industry has gotten hot, and business forecasters expect it to boom even more in the coming decade. Kimmins Environmental Service specializes in garbage and construction site cleanups as well as wrecking projects that clear sites of old buildings to make way for new construction. They also handle toxic waste disposal and numerous other environmental cleanup jobs. Business has been booming at Kimmins, with 1990 revenues of over $25 million and with a goal of $300 to $500 million within the next five years.

However, Kimmins's customers have been complaining that the company's services do not match the standards identified in the firm's contracts and mandated by the industry and the government. One customer, a St. Louis-based metals and reclamation firm, hired Kimmins to demolish three foundry buildings and haul off the wreckage. However, the firm recently filed suit against Kimmins, claiming that Kimmins not only took much longer than expected to do the job, but, in fact, buried the debris on the site. Kimmins's chairman and CEO, Francis Williams, admitted that wood had been buried on the location, but an excavation of the site revealed much more: scrap metal, trash, metal drums with toxic wastes, and more. Other customers have complained about Kimmins as well, charging that the company does not adhere sufficiently to environmental safeguards and standards and that its cleanups are unsafe and far from what the company promises. Some Kimmins projects have had to be halted because of the poor and dangerous quality of the haphazard services. Selling below-standard services is bad business in the long term, and no company can continue to get away with it.

❧ The Key Question

How do you avoid selling and delivering below-standard products or services?

Kimmins's Answer

Some people have accused Kimmins Environmental Service of being out of control. Fran Williams refutes that charge. He suggests that continued growth in his industry will be easy and that he fully expects to make a lot of money in the next few years. Maybe so. Maybe not. Under an $11 million contract with Manville Corporation to remove the asbestos from 16 old manufacturing facilities and then demolish the buildings, Kimmins again ran afoul of standards. From the beginning, Manville and the engineering firm it hired to supervise the job found Kimmins violating safety requirements and operating below contract and industry standards. After shutting the project down twice in its early stages, Kimmins still refused to meet standards and ultimately lost the contract. Now Kimmins has sued Manville for inappropriate termination. What does Fran Williams have to say about all of this complaining from customers? As reported in both local and national media, Williams simply says, "We didn't do a good job" and then, shrugging, adds, "It happens." Despite such apparent disregard for standards of quality required by contracts and the industry, Kimmins seems to believe it can continue to grow aggressively in the years to come. It may be in for a bit of a shock, however, since providing below-standard products or services may make you rich in the short term but will surely hurt you in the long term.

Suggested Right Answers

Below are a few points to help you avoid ever selling or delivering anything below standard:

1. *Raise your standard of quality above that of the industry's average.*

2. *Put your standards higher than customers expect.*

3. *Never succumb to the short-term temptation of selling a prod-*

uct or service below standard, even if you think your customers will accept it.

4. **If you want to sell a product or service to a customer segment that requires a lower level of quality and lower set of standards, then separate that product or service offering from higher-standard offerings.**

5. **Never inventory rejected or below-standard products as a means to meet potential excessive demand.**

6. **Never reduce manpower or expertise requirements on a job in order to take on more business elsewhere.**

7. **If anything does get through below standard, make sure you correct it quickly, at your own expense, not your customers'.**

Applying Right Answers

Two construction companies in the southeast recently entered Chapter 11 bankruptcy proceedings but for very different reasons. These two companies had competed against one another from time to time, but generally their strategies took them into different markets. I'll refer to these two companies as Steenblik Construction and Leland Construction. Steenblik Construction focused on the higher-quality construction market, building some of the most elegant and beautiful structures in the southeast. Leland Construction focused on the lowest-cost market, keeping costs down while erecting buildings that would still meet a customer's needs. Steenblik Construction got into trouble by continually exceeding construction budgets by such enormous amounts that it finally outran its customers' patience. Steenblik used the highest-quality materials and always made its customers proud, if not poor. Most recently, Steenblik had overrun the budget by a full 50 percent for a $100 million office building. The building was gorgeous, but the company's client refused to pay for the budget overrun, thus sending Steenblik into Chapter 11.

Leland Construction, on the other hand, had also built a lot of buildings that initially pleased customers, but because Leland cut corners on the quality of materials in order to achieve low costs, it eventually tried its customers' patience, too. Difficulties with some of their buildings generated such negative press that Leland found itself unable to gain new contracts. Leland also sought protection under Chapter 11 when it could no longer meet overhead expenses.

Oddly enough, Steenblik Construction had positioned itself so that no one could ever accuse it of doing the sort of shoddy work that brought down Leland Construction. Unfortunately, Steenblik went too far, and in an effort to avoid any below-standard selling or delivery, it nearly drove itself out of business. Leland Construction never made it out of Chapter 11 and eventually moved into Chapter 7 liquidation. Fortunately, however, Steenblik Construction learned from its mistakes and after a three-year period succeeded in pulling out of Chapter 11. Now Steenblik provides a level of quality in its construction projects that meets or slightly exceeds industry and customer expectations. Selling below-quality standards may bring you short-term results, but it will almost always compromise your long-term health. In your endeavors to make sure that you deliver above-quality standards, however, you don't want to become so fanatic that you overburden your company, and in that fashion also impair results.

Part III
SERVICE

11

Do You Segment Markets by Service Expectation?

&

A neighbor was strolling through a local crafts fair when a display caught her eye. The craftswoman, primarily a calligrapher, was selling a variety of tote bags, wall plaques, loose-leaf binders, folders, and other commonly used items. For a few dollars, she would customize one of the products with a name, a phrase, a logo, or a picture. Even though our neighbor had seen similar displays before, she was extremely impressed with how this craftswoman seemed to perfectly blend her customizing calligraphy with a few basic products that everyone used. The neighbor purchased several items, including a tote bag for my wife, which she brought over that evening along with a persuasive invitation to not miss the display at the crafts fair.

As my wife and I reflected on our neighbor's enthusiasm, we couldn't help discussing how hungry most people are for products and services customized to their specific needs. Such customizing can make all the difference in a buying decision.

Big business can learn a valuable lesson from that calligrapher's customizing service, one that works just as effectively in computer software as it does in novelty items. Competition has gotten brutal in the computer software industry, with giants like Microsoft and Lotus waging a pitched battle for customers. With billions of dollars in revenues and over 5200 employees, Microsoft has been winning the war, partly because it has worked so hard to differentiate one customer's needs from another's. As the use of computers has spread and become more sophisticated, customers have naturally become more and more specific about the kinds of programs and applications they expect from software companies. Strategically, Microsoft has wisely chosen to respond to this increased segmentation by investing a good deal of time looking for ways to satisfy individualized and customized needs. Specifically, Microsoft has decided to provide more and more specialized consulting services in the future, charging customers for their aid in developing unique programs and applications.

‌‌The Key Question

How do you accurately identify and effectively satisfy the different service expectations of your customers?

Microsoft's Answer

Microsoft has recently signed contracts with over 3000 new clients who need customized applications and special working features in their programs. These targeted customers have responded enthusiastically to Microsoft's intention of helping them tailor software to their unique needs. To help identify and deliver such specialized programs, Microsoft has hired a former executive from Ernst & Young to head up their consulting service. Robert McDowell, in turn, has set about hiring a group of 300 consultants around the country whose job will be to determine the service expectations and needs of new market segments. This represents a big investment, if not a big gamble. Whether it ultimately pays off or not, we won't know for a few years, but one thing is certain, Microsoft Consulting Services has stepped out in front of its competitors in the area of segmenting markets by service expectation.

Suggested Right Answers

In order to segment your customers based upon service expectations, think about doing the following:

1. *Recognize that in a service-dominated society, whether you're selling products or services, segmenting customer groups and markets will depend more and more on determining service expectations.*

2. *Marshal the necessary internal forces to define the service expectations of your customers.*

3. *Increase your research into how customers use the services, whether core or peripheral, you offer.*

4. *Be prepared to further customize your services, even in seemingly minor ways.*

5. *Consider offering a cafeteria-plan of services to your customers as a means of more effectively segmenting and addressing expectations.*

Applying Right Answers

A partner (I'll call her Diane) in a small tax consulting firm provided a full range of tax services to clients, from the completion of tax forms to sophisticated financial planning. She had spent 10 years in this staid industry and had never viewed her marketplace as anything but a big general market. Oh, she worried about meeting the specific needs of quite a few different clients, but as she and her partners began to encounter increased competition from other firms in the area, she concluded that her company needed a new edge. Could she find new ways to segment their clients, better identifying the services unique individuals might expect? If so, should they recruit special talent that could perfectly satisfy those expectations?

To answer these and related questions, Diane organized a partners' retreat that would focus on strategic market segmentation and future staffing requirements. At the beginning of the full-day session, Diane and her three partners stated that, "the goal of this retreat will be to figure out the specific kinds of clients we want to attract and design service inducements that will get them into our office and keep them there."

As the group of partners worked toward this goal, they identified other services that they had habitually considered tangential to the basic service of preparing tax returns. As they did so, they discovered even more "tangential" services than they had ever imagined, with the list including everything from investment counseling to training in a variety of record keeping and budgeting skills. They talked at length about each of their important clients, trying in each case to isolate a service opportunity that might make a client undyingly loyal. In the end, they were able to identify six basic groups of clients with somewhat unique service expectations. These six groups became their targets. Getting them into the office and keeping them there would require hiring two new specialists, one in the area of estate and retirement planning and one in the area of family-owned businesses. The plan went into effect, and in the following year, the firm attained a 25 percent increase in new clients simply because their service offerings were so uniquely attractive. Even in a service business, Diane discovered it makes a lot of sense to segment customers into ever-finer niches, according to their unique service expectations.

12

Are You Providing the Service Customers Want?

ᴥ

As part of a weekend getaway, my wife and I found ourselves in a fine restaurant, enjoying the ambiance and looking forward to a delicious meal. As we surveyed the menu and made our selections, we were surprised by all the "extras" that came with the entree: a drink, appetizer, sorbet, salad, vegetables, and dessert. When the waiter approached our table to take our orders, I asked him if I could trade my salad for a cup of mushroom soup, and he emphatically said, "No." Shocked, I asked, "Why not?" Shaking his head, he said such a trade would violate house policy. Later, my wife observed how inconsistent that policy seemed to be with the reputation, atmosphere, and quality of the restaurant.

Her comments got me to thinking about how, like this restaurant, so many companies try to force their customers and clients to accept the services the companies deem most valuable rather than responding to customers' desires.

In the car rental business, competitors have raced to capture their shares of the multi-billion-dollar business travel market. To business people, you must offer services beyond those offered to the regular tourist. The big four in the market, Hertz, Avis, National, and Budget have battled one another to make their services meet the needs of business people, offering everything from special corporate rates to express check-in and return, conveniently located parking lots, and customer counters in airports. As these companies vie for business travelers each year, you can see dozens of examples of new customer services.

Enter Alamo Rental Car, which saw a market segment that was being neglected by the big four: the "ordinary" tourist. In order to attract this market, Alamo knew it would have to develop a set of services geared to its specific needs. A key factor for tourists would clearly be price, and that one factor would probably outweigh the many other services provided by Hertz, Avis, National, and Budget. To effect low prices, Alamo located its operations away from airports and only in high-traffic markets, a move that mitigated against the quick check-in, express return, and easy access touted by the big four. For Alamo to serve the ordinary tourist it became a matter of eliminating services offered to business travelers.

❧ The Key Question

How do you make sure your culture and organizational capabilities match the service needs of your customers?

Alamo's Answer

As a relative newcomer to the car rental business, Alamo knew early on that it would have trouble competing with the big four, so it looked for alternatives. In doing so, it identified a trend that has continued over recent years: the growth of the leisure market for rental cars. In fact, the leisure market has been expanding in recent years at twice that of the business traveler market. Alamo built its whole organization and culture around its market, purposefully excluding many of the conveniences and services that appeal to business travelers. Alamo does not earn high marks for customer satisfaction when compared to the big four car rental companies. However, such comparisons matter little to Alamo's culture because most customer satisfaction surveys in the industry are based on business travel customers and not the leisure customers, who don't care as much about Alamo's relative lack of services. Alamo would rather score points with cost-conscious tourists. In order to score those points, Alamo has adopted a new program called "Best Friends," aimed at providing courteous and friendly service to individuals and families on vacations.

Alamo will probably never compete toe-to-toe with Hertz, Avis, and the others, but that doesn't seem to bother Alamo, which enjoys picking up the market sub-segments that the big companies disdain. Today, Alamo enjoys revenues of over $500 million a year, ranking it Number 5 among the rental car companies. Its profits come in second among the 11 car rental companies—better than Hertz, National, and Budget.

Suggested Right Answers

As you develop your organizational culture to become ever more sensitive to your customers' service needs, consider the following:

1. *Match your organizational culture with the service needs of your customers, even if that means promoting sub-cultures within your organization.*

2. *When going after a new target customer segment that requires different services, don't attempt to do it with the same culture or sub-culture that serves other segments.*

3. *Remember that the most effective cultures do not try to be all things to all service segments.*

Applying Right Answers

The vice president of field services for a medium-sized valve manufacturing company (I'll call him Jack) worked hard to serve customers in the oil and chemical business who required the most
sophisticated process components available. To meet their needs,
Jack had developed a range of services that his technical support
people offered to their customers, ranging from engineering, design, and installation services to overnight shipping capability.
He urged his people in field services to be ready at any time to
provide any of the services their customers might need, and he
prided himself on being able to respond to even the most unusual
needs.

Unfortunately, his zeal sometimes led him to imagine needs that
didn't even exist, a tendency that greatly frustrated his people.
A typical scenario occurred when the sales people made rather
nonspecific promises of unlimited service that did not take into
account what a given customer really wanted. As a result, installation people would show up at a customer's door, only to
find out that the customer did not want installation help. On other
occasions, customized valves did not suit the needs of the customer because design services people had not been involved. For
his part, Jack just chalked up any problems to the normal "mis-
communications" that were a natural part of doing business in
this industry.

Over the years, however, the culture in Jack's department became
schizophrenic. Because the organization never knew precisely
what customers demanded in terms of services, it never knew
exactly how to staff different functions within the company, nor
could it be certain that it was ever delivering the right kind or
level of service. All this led to a confused and fragmented organizational culture, always at odds with the service needs of its
customers.

Even when this problem became acute with high turnover and

declining productivity, Jack refused to acknowledge its serious-ness. Not until the company had lost a number of its key custom-ers to competitors did he even feel a need to look into the situation. Eventually the senior management team sought outside help to find the root causes behind lost business. After a particularly strenuous investigation, the senior team reached a decision to divide the company into three groups functioning as separate divisions. One group catered to those customers who needed engineering design help to create unique processing valves for their manufacturing processes. Another group focused on those customers who needed construction design and installation as-sistance, and the third group tackled customers with their own design and installation capabilities who usually wanted speedy delivery.

The company's ability to meet the service needs of its key seg-ments beyond the provision of the basic valves that the company produced was greatly enhanced by this separation. The confusion and mixed signals that had frustrated the culture for so long now largely vanished as each division developed a culture matched to the service needs of its particular customers. Jack discovered that success in the valve manufacturing business stemmed as much from tailoring its services as from producing quality products.

13

Should You Change the Type or Level of Service You Provide?

෨

A few years ago, my youngest daughter and I went shopping at a local grocery store—not the one where our family usually shops—and my daughter said, "Why don't they have ice cream and drinks like they do at the other store?" I said, "Sweetheart, they just don't." She then asked, "Why not?" I answered, "Not all stores are the same." Again, she asked, "Why not?" All I could say was, "We'll stop on the way home and get you an ice cream cone, okay?" She clapped her hands, "Okay." However, this brief interchange caused me to think about the many, many different services that companies add to and subtract from the basic commodities, merchandise, or services that they sell in an effort to meet customer needs and increase their business. What an enormous task faces businesspeople as they try to decide how and when to change their peripheral services.

Linda Wachner is CEO of Warnaco, the $650 million apparel distribution company that sells Christian Dior, Hathaway, Olga, and other brand-name merchandise to upscale department stores, boutiques, and specialty stores around the country. Since Warnaco's customers consist of retailers in a highly competitive retailing environment, Warnaco must keep on its toes in terms of the kind and level of services it provides. Added pressure on

Linda Wachner and Warnaco comes from the debt financing she incurred as a result of a leveraged buyout by management in the late 1980s. As a result, no one at Warnaco can afford to make mistakes and still hope for the company to remain in business. The key to success? More and better customer service.

To do so, Linda Wachner and her people geared up their sales force to provide additional help to retailers, such as making sure that the merchandise is displayed alluringly and that sufficient quantities are on hand to meet the needs of shoppers. Warnaco sales people began helping retailers sell the merchandise by answering consumers' questions and providing all-around merchandising support. In addition, Linda Wachner and seven of her key executives visited Carter Hawley Hale, Allied Federated, May, and other big retailers in 1990 to find out just what additional services they might offer. Such willingness to adjust services, as needed, won the allegiance of both the retailers and end consumers.

❧ *The Key Question*

How and when do you decide to change the type and level of service you provide your customers?

Warnaco's Answer

In the apparel business, since fashion rules the day, you must effectively respond to trends. Linda Wachner views changing service levels in the very same way. She's always ready to change the way she sells, the way she organizes her sales force, or anything else to provide better service to retailers. For example, in 1991 Warnaco augmented its sales force significantly in order to provide even more sales assistance to retail stores. This "above and beyond the call of duty" approach to customer service should improve Warnaco's own bottom line. For Linda

Wachner, the idea of service never strays very far from the concept of change.

Suggested Right Answers

The following tips may help you get a better handle on changing types and levels of service:

1. *Regularly evaluate the types and levels of service provided by your competitors.*

2. *Constantly ask your customers about new types and levels of service they might appreciate.*

3. *Study other industries for clues to service changes you might adopt to your own industry.*

4. *Always monitor customer response to any changes you make, and be prepared to make decisive adjustments.*

Applying Right Answers

Deciding how and when to add services or change the level of existing service can pose a real problem in any market or industry, but the decisions become especially timely when it comes to selling automobiles. The son of the founder of a dozen different car dealerships spread out over an entire region of the western United States (I'll call him Allen), convinced his father to let him run one of them by himself. Eager to impress his father, Allen decided to distinguish his dealership by radically changing service levels and adding a whole host of new services. Unfortunately, he did so with too little thought or analysis. With four different franchises under one roof, his dealership would automatically sell more cars, he assumed, if it gave customers more service. Within a few weeks of his taking over the dealership, he was offering car buyers life-time oil change service and free tune-ups every other year.

During the first year of these new services, competitors shook their heads over Allen's apparent stupidity and the state of his father's pockets. Of course, customers valued the new service after they purchased a car at Allen's but as the dealership moved into the second year under Allen's leadership, it became painfully obvious that these new services were not really motivating customers to buy cars. In addition, the new services had drained the black ink from the dealership's bottom line. At the end of two years, the dealership curtailed the policy, biting the bullet by continuing the oil change and tune-up pledge to hundreds of customers who had purchased cars during the first two years of Allen's tenure.

Allen learned the hard way that he needed to think twice before leaping to change services. The magnitude of the changes he had introduced had backfired because competitors had told customers it was "too good to be true" and the dealership would never be able to keep it up. When Allen suspended the policy, the competitors naturally used it against Allen. One competitor even proclaimed in his TV advertising, "We don't play tricks with service to get your business."

Now when Allen thinks about making changes in the types and levels of service, he first monitors any changes among his competitors, directly seeks his customer's advice about what they want, and weighs the probable impact of any proposed change on customers' decisions to buy an automobile. He carefully tests new service and promotion ideas with focus groups and selected customers before implementing them dealership-wide. As a result of all this, Allen has reinstituted the policy of free oil changes, with the qualification that this does not include the oil or the oil filter, only the labor. This modification has proven to be both attractive to customers and less draining on profits. The customer may always be right, Allen now knows, but that doesn't mean that unlimited customer service is always right.

14

Who Assumes Responsibility for Service?

࿊

*H*ave you ever gone into an office, a government agency, a store, or some other place of business and become totally frustrated by being passed around from one person to another to get what you want? This age-old problem can plague even the best organizations and institutions in this era of customer service.

Recently, I went to the library of a top-notch university, seeking some rather obscure research material and in the process heard at least four times that I would have to talk to somebody else to get that information. In each case, the line went something like, "That's not my area. I can't help you; try so and so." I found myself feeling sorry for the students who used this library every day and wondered whether or not the problem I encountered didn't partly explain why many college students don't do a very good job of writing and research.

As I left the library, I thought how different my experience might have been if everyone I had talked to had taken upon themselves the responsibility to provide good service. What if the first person I talked to had gone out of his way to take me through the maze? When everyone in an organization does take it upon himself or herself to provide exceptional service, that can produce an awesome power in the marketplace.

One of the most heralded examples of making sure everyone in an organization assumes responsibility for service can be found at the Scandinavian Airline System. Considered one of the best airlines in the world, SAS has won numerous awards over the past few years from various trade publications and organizations. When Jan Carlzon took over the airline in 1981, it was losing money. One year later, it was again profitable, and it has seen steady growth and profits ever since. Carlzon's strategy to position SAS as one of the best airlines in the world was simple: "We want to be the preferred airline for the frequent business traveler." To this end, every improvement he has made at SAS has addressed the needs of the business traveler, and only the business traveler. SAS arranges scheduling to provide frequent flights, with many nonstops that appeal to harried business people. To facilitate changeovers, SAS situates its planes in such a way that business travelers don't have to run across another concourse to make connecting flights but, rather, only move to a gate right next to the one they just exited. The company is even designing planes in a joint project with Boeing to create cabin improvements that will please passengers, and it has formed transfer and hub-sharing alliances with airlines worldwide to ease the connections global travelers must make.

ᨭ The Key Question

How do you get everyone in your organization to become more service oriented?

SAS's Answer

The ultimate responsibility for implementing Carlzon's strategy to win the business traveler lies with all of the front-line employees at SAS. Carlzon restructured SAS so that the entire management structure could support all employees, such as ticket agents, flight attendants, and all those who come in contact with passengers each day. Carlzon estimates that more than 50,000 "moments of truth" occur for SAS each day—15-second intervals in which a business traveler interacts with an SAS employee and forms an impression of the company. Jan Carlzon wrote a book called *Moments of Truth* in the English edition but *Destroying the Pyramid* in Swedish. According to Carlzon, the company had to ensure that each "moment of truth" would win a loyal customer. To do so, he eliminated lengthy procedures, work rules, and supervisory approval (pyramids) so that every front-line employee could assume the authority to make key decisions and solve problems for their customers on the spot. He reasons that if a company must convey a customer's need up an organizational hierarchy, the 15-second opportunity will elapse, and the chance to serve a customer will be lost forever.

Under Carlzon's new organizational system, no customer should embark on a flight with an unresolved worry or problem. In an anecdote that Carlzon loves to relate, a purser on a delayed flight across Sweden decided to compensate the passengers for the inconvenience by providing them with free snacks and drinks that had not been scheduled as part of the flight. When airport SAS food officials balked, she circumvented them, took responsibility for the situation herself, and managed to obtain the food by paying for it out of her petty cash fund. In situations like this, people demonstrate the importance of Jan Carlzon's unusual management approach.

Suggested Right Answers

The following tips can help your employees become more responsible for the service they provide:

1. *Teach your people to believe that every contact with a customer offers a golden opportunity to provide service.*

2. *Streamline your organizational structure to give every employee the opportunity, flexibility, and encouragement to provide the service that customers need at the moment.*

3. *Make sure your management processes and systems increase rather than hinder personal effectiveness in customer interactions.*

4. *Help the people in your organization understand that the small things that happen day after day and accumulate over time make the biggest difference to long-term success.*

5. *Conduct surveys, focus groups, or interviews with the employees in your organization at least annually to determine whether they feel they are personally effective in meeting the service needs of your customers.*

6. *Whenever you find individuals who feel they are not personally effective or feel they are not responsible for service, resolve that problem immediately.*

Applying Right Answers

The manager of a branch bank in a small city (I'll call her Gayle) worked for a large banking company headquartered nearby in a major metropolitan area. Since her company had been stressing personalized customer service that would allow the bank to survive the extreme difficulties of the early 1990s, the bank company president sent copies of Jan Carlzon's *Moments of Truth* to every branch and department manager, asking everyone to read it carefully and pass it along to employees under their supervision. After reading the book, Gayle became convinced that she could greatly help her people feel more responsible for providing individual service. She herself began to look for opportunities to provide the sort of extraordinary service that would ensure customer loyalty, and she encouraged everyone under her to do likewise. It turned out to be more easily said than done, however, until a genuine "moment of truth" arrived.

It was late July, and Gayle was under the gun to get her monthly reports completed and submitted to the corporate office. In the midst of this pressure, one of her loan officers (I'll call him Ted), walked into her office with a thorny problem. One of the branch's customers, on vacation in Europe, had to make an unscheduled pay off on a personal note held by another bank. This customer had changed banks a year earlier specifically because of Gayle's bank's advertised focus on personalized attention. At the moment, no one at the customer's business or home could help the bank track him down, but if he did not make the required payment, he could suffer a financial penalty, not to mention a possible lawsuit. The other bank had, of course, taken a dim view of the customer's defection and would not likely feel much sympathy for his problem. While the customer had sufficient funds in his account to cover the payment, without his authorization neither Gayle nor Ted could tap those funds.

Gayle and Ted sprang into action, hoping to find some way to reach their customer in Europe. After numerous calls, they located a relative who knew where their customer was staying in the south of France. The next morning, after several overseas calls, Gayle and Ted finally reached the customer, not in France but in Spain. The customer, both embarrassed and grateful, wired authorization for the necessary payment. Ted personally walked the check over to the other bank, meeting the customer's obligation with only an hour to spare. Gayle again called the customer in Europe to reassure him that everything was fine. "I don't know how to thank you," he said. Gayle laughed, "Just banking with us is all the thanks we need."

This story became a legend at Gayle's company, and over time, dozens more were added to it as people strove to emulate Gayle's and Ted's going above and beyond the call of duty to serve a customer. Gayle's branch and the entire bank have greatly benefitted from many "moments of truth," with growth and earnings rising well above the troubled industry's averages.

15

What Does Service Really Do for You?

&

A friend of mine owns a distribution company that publishes a fairly elaborate newsletter once a month, updating its customers on inventory levels and new merchandise. In the course of casual conversation one day, I asked him why he kept doing it.

"Oh, we've done it for as long as I can remember."

When I asked him what his customers thought of it, he replied, "I don't know."

"Do they use it to order products?"

"No."

"Is the information in it really critical for their decision making?"

"No, our salesmen keep in weekly contact with most of our customers."

"How much does it cost you to put this newsletter out?"

"About $5000 a month."

"What would happen if you discontinued it?"

"Nothing."

"Do it."

"What?"

"Discontinue the newsletter, and give the $60,000 you'll save annually to charity. It will do you more good."

I was half joking, but it's no joke that corporate America wastes a lot of its resources providing services nobody wants or needs. Eliminating those services could permit far more productive use of those squandered dollars.

Century Health Care is a $100 million company that provides psychiatric care to adolescents. It was founded by Jerry Dillon, a man who himself grew up in a boys' home and who feels a deep commitment to help young people struggling with emotional and psychological problems. The company has expanded from its original base in Tulsa, Oklahoma, and now operates facilities throughout the country.

As the company grew and strove to maintain a leadership position in the field, it felt a constant pressure to offer more and new services to meet its patients' needs. As services proliferated, Century promoted key legislation that would allow insurance coverage and other government subsidies to defray a family's costs. Despite its efforts, however, many families simply could not afford the full room, board, and curriculum expenses. Century Health Care found itself in a real financial dilemma—wanting to provide top-flight services but stymied by the lack of sufficient insurance coverage to pay for those services.

❧ The Key Question

What results are your services really producing?

Century Health Care's Answer

In the late 1980s, Jerry Dillon and Tom Kelly, Century's president and chief operating officer, along with other Century executives, including operations vice president Tim Welsh decided to focus on a reduced set of services for the majority of patients in order to achieve a better match between costs and insurance coverage. While the company would still offer its full-care program, it would eliminate certain services that were beyond the budgets of the vast majority of families.

As a result, many of Century Health Care's facilities have now become outpatient service centers where adolescents come only during the day for treatment, study, and help but return to their homes for meals and shelter. In this way, Century Health not only contains costs but is trying to improve upon the benefits its patients can derive from family living. The scaled-down services get better results given the constraints of insurance coverage and patients' financial resources. Unfortunately, Century Health Care didn't move fast enough to avoid some serious financial difficulties. Both Tom Kelly and Tim Welsh left the company in early 1991, and Jerry Dillon is still scaling back services to return the company to profitability.

Suggested Right Answers

As you weigh which services to add, eliminate, or maintain in your own organization, ask yourself the following questions:

1. *Rank your services according to the value your customers place on them. Study each, especially those lower on the scale, and*

*ask yourself if they really increase your competitiveness or
results.*

2. *Do the same for your key competitors. Do they offer services
you do not offer? Do such services greatly increase their competitiveness in the market or their bottom line results?*

3. *When setting long-term goals and evaluating long-term results,
closely examine three lists of services: those you must maintain, those you might add, and those you might eliminate.*

4. *Always use long-term results as the basis for deciding which
services to add, subtract, or maintain.*

Applying Right Answers

A Southern California entrepreneur (I'll call him Louis) recently
started a new kind of a la carte restaurant based upon a "no-frills"
approach to customer service. What is a restaurant, figured Louis,
but a place to cook and eat food? Convinced that the economy
was fast approaching a point where increasing levels of personal
service and the high costs associated with them would put fancier
establishments out of business, Louis decided to let his patrons
cook their own food on grills or in ovens or frying vats. It was a
sort of "home away from home" kitchen, with all the basics, from
basic meats, vegetables, fruits, and spices to cooking equipment
provided. For example, a customer could come in and deep-fry
two shrimp, sauté a few mushrooms, and visit the salad bar,
paying only for what he used or consumed.

The customers received clear instructions and safety warnings,
but if they burned their shrimp, they still paid for it. Louis's
restaurant became enormously popular with a number of regular
customers, who constantly suggested new ingredients and appliances. Louis responded by offering a reservation service that
would allow a customer to call in a day ahead and ask for certain

ingredients and utensils to be on hand for a particular date and time. By eliminating most of the usual (and costly) services associated with a restaurant—taking orders, waiting on tables, mixing drinks, providing refills, cooking food, and cleaning up—Louis could charge much lower prices and offer his customers tremendous flexibility in terms of exactly what they wanted to eat. Well, Louis's restaurant may have struck a lot of people as downright weird, but the word spread and Louis now plans to open a second restaurant. Will the concept catch on throughout the country? Who knows? But one thing is for sure, Louis has figured out how to eliminate services in order to get results. As the economy dictates against the proliferation of increases in services, Louis won't be the only person finding a silver lining in an otherwise dark cloud.

Part IV

ADVANTAGE

❧

16

Do You Fully Exploit Your Competitive Advantages?

---------- è& ----------

Competitive advantage. It's such a simple concept but such a hard one to practice. I had just finished writing a proposal for a new book and decided to get it printed, not at the usual copy shop but at a specialty printer that had done a number of quality projects for me over the years. As I was waiting for my material to be bound, I chatted with the owner about his business. He moaned and grumbled about how competitive the market had become, but then he added, "There is one bright spot. We've developed an embossing process that will produce better quality at half the price." I asked him whether that process served a growing need and, surprisingly, he said, "I don't know." His people had developed the process about a year and a half ago, but since few customers wanted embossing, it represented a small portion of his business. When I asked him how many of his customers knew about it, he replied, "I don't really push it." Before I left the shop, I told the owner, "I'd say you've got a potential competitive advantage in your embossing services, but if I were you, I'd make sure everybody in town hears about it." He waved and said, "Maybe next year." As I drove home, I thought about all the other companies that fail to fully exploit their advantages.

The name Gucci stands for high fashion and exclusivity—at least until recently. The Italian fashion designer and retailer has long enjoyed a competitive advantage as an elite marketer of high-quality, limited-quantity fashion goods and accessories. The name itself became synonymous with exclusive fashion and design in clothing and accessories to millions of consumers around the world. Such a competitive advantage is not easy to come by, but if you begin to misunderstand or misinterpret the true essence of that advantage, you can lose it quickly.

Gucci had preserved its image by limiting its outlets and products worldwide. But during the 1980s, that careful focus on the company's competitive advantage virtually disappeared in the wake of intense family squabbling. Quarreling factions within the Gucci family created separate centers of power within the company, with little or no coordination between them. As a result, no one paid attention to protecting the company's prized competitive advantage—the exclusivity of its name and reputation. As a result of this internal strife, the elegant Gucci shops wildly grew in number to over 2500, and the number of other outlets selling Gucci products exploded to several thousand. The Gucci name and trademark were licensed so indiscriminately, it soon appeared on more than 14,000 products, from sheets and towels to T-shirts and inexpensive, low-quality watches. The sudden proliferation of Gucci products turned the company's image almost overnight into one as commonplace as J.C. Penney. Some marketing consultants and analysts even began to disparage the once-elegant Gucci symbol itself as an emblem of schlock.

❧ The Key Question

Do you make wise strategic choices about developing and sustaining competitive advantages?

Gucci's Answer

Maurizio Gucci, once the president of Gucci but eventually only the leader of one of the family factions, decided that the company could only save itself by pursuing a single strategy built around the goal of recapturing and rebuilding the company's most important competitive advantage—its image and reputation. First, the squabbling had to stop. With the backing of a Bahrain-based investment banking firm, Maurizio obtained the muscle to regain the uncontested presidency of Gucci. The investment bank held a 50 percent stake in Gucci after it bought out all the squabbling family factions. Maurizio himself seized the reins and began buying back franchises around the world and tightening control over Gucci's fast-growing Asian operations. In addition, he started slashing the number of retailers permitted to merchandise Gucci products from several thousand to just 500 specially appointed outlets. The scaling back of Gucci products continues while, at the same time, the company has hired famed designer and retailer Dawn Mello to head up product development. Not surprisingly, the strategy seems to be paying off already, as Gucci has reclaimed a good deal of its exclusive heritage.

Suggested Right Answers

In order to improve your strategic decisions regarding competitive advantages, consider the following steps:

1. *Define your competitive advantages specifically and precisely.*

2. *Based on customer feedback, research, and observed behavior, determine whether the world perceives your competitive advantages the same way you do.*

3. *Once you have identified and verified your key competitive advantages, make sure you understand them fully.*

4. *Never make a strategic decision without calculating its impact on your competitive advantages.*

5. *Make sure that your key competitive advantages drive the development of your strategy.*

Applying Right Answers

An electronics buff (I'll call him Dennis) quit college in the middle of his junior year to start his own TV repair service. Rather than start from scratch, however, Dennis bought an existing service from its retiring owner. Dennis couldn't resist the opportunity, since he'd always loved tinkering with electronics and dreamed of a future when, as head of his own company, he'd be repairing and servicing all kinds of electronic products.

Dennis studied business in college and had especially enjoyed the subject of business strategies. Of course, when it came time to develop a strategy for his own business, he paid careful attention to his company's potential competitive advantages. After thinking long and hard about this issue, he formulated his company's motto: "We can fix anything and save you money in the process." To deliver this promise, Dennis envisioned an organization with multiple locations that would buy component parts at a discount and hire the best possible technicians—people who shared his own passion for tinkering.

Dennis also realized that his company would have to fix a customer's TV, stero, or VCR for significantly less than the cost of a new one. This necessity would put pressure on effective cost control and the creative tinkering of his people. As the years went by, Dennis never gave up that initial conception of his company's competitive advantage, and his vision of multiple locations and a strong reputation for being able to fix anything at a reasonable price became a reality. Much of Dennis's success sprang from his dogged and unwavering commitment to the competitive advantage he wanted to establish for his company.

At one point, about five years into his company's development,

Dennis faced a real crisis. With three stores and 10 technicians in place, he was beginning to make even stronger promises to the public. An aggressive advertising campaign guaranteed customers that Dennis's company could fix any electronic product cheaper than it would cost to buy a new one. As the advertising campaign ran its course on radio and in local newspapers, hundreds of customers brought in old TVs, stereos, and appliances that hadn't worked for years, expecting Dennis to deliver on that promise. The resulting debacle almost capsized the business, but Dennis delivered, even though in some cases it meant buying products and selling them to customers for less than they could buy them elsewhere. Still, Dennis weathered the crisis and established his firm as the most technically competent and service-oriented appliance repair company in the region. Dennis's determination to hold on to his company's hard-won competitive advantage has continued to serve his company so well he now owns 45 service outlets in four metropolitan areas.

17

Do Your Advantages Match Your Values?

❧

One of our children cornered me when she came home from school one day and said, "My art teacher thinks that I have real talent." As it turned out, her teacher had suggested we invest in private art lessons. But when I asked my daughter, "Do you *want* to take art lessons?" she paused before answering, "No, I really don't like it that much." As she bounced off to call one of her friends to play, I wondered how often people do things just because they do them well, even when they don't really enjoy doing them. They usually end up miserable. Companies, too, oftentimes develop advantages that don't match their cultural values or they hold cultural values that don't align well with current advantages. That sort of mismatch also courts misery.

Systematic Management Services provides project management and control services for major federal government agencies such as the Department of Energy and the Department of Defense, as well as for some private companies such as Boeing, Martin Marietta, and the New York Airport Authority. SMS was founded by Dil Kulkarni, a man who left India 20 years ago with the dream of building a successful company in the United States. Having gained some initial disappointing experience with other government contractors, Dil Kulkarni decided to build his own company around a different set of values in an industry where many organizations feel no compunction over thrusting their hands into deep government funding pockets. Dil, who found that attitude unacceptable, vowed not to operate as a so-called "beltway bandit" (a name given to some questionable government contractors traveling the beltway around Washington, D.C.), quick to take the government's money with too little regard for the quality of service delivered.

In 1975, Dil Kulkarni built Systematic Management Services around the deeply felt values of integrity, quality of service, and surpassing customer expectations. These values ran so against the grain in the government contracting industry that it took employees, not to mention customers, a long time to appreciate Dil Kulkarni's approach. Gradually, however, many, including executives in the Department of Energy, came to recognize that Dil Kulkarni's word and service promise were as good as gold. SMS employees began to enjoy this different kind of environment, and many of them broke the typical pattern of moving from one government contractor to the next as the contracts changed hands.

❧ *The Key Question*

Can you turn strongly felt values into advantages or hard-won advantages into values?

SMS's Answer

Dil Kulkarni's and SMS's values began to translate into key advantages in the marketplace. As the company grew, Dil Kulkarni felt a need to formulate the company's values even more concretely. As a result, he identified seven basic values for the organization, each starting with a "C." The "Seven C's" included: Competence, Conscience, Consistency, Commitment, Communication, Cooperation, and Compassion, and they became woven into every organizational activity, from management retreats, performance appraisals, company communications, and hiring practices to the proposal process and communications with clients and customers. These values, becoming more and more embedded throughout the organization of some 200 professionals and staff, allowed the company to develop two key advantages: first, the ability to attract and maintain good, competent people, and second, the ability to deliver promised quality and service to clients. These advantages, in turn, have helped SMS win major jobs with the Department of Energy and other federal government agencies. In several cases, SMS stood side by side with Rockwell International, Boeing, Martin Marietta, Bechtel, and other major government contractors as a prime contractor on a significant project. In many other cases, SMS provided project control services that involved monitoring these other large contractors.

Driven by values, the SMS culture has developed some hard-won advantages in a highly competitive marketplace. Now SMS is expanding beyond government contracting into private sector consulting and international construction management services, arenas in which SMS's strong set of values should work just as well.

Suggested Right Answers

When you try to match values and advantages, you should consider the following:

1. *Matching values and advantages is usually a two-step process.*

2. *If values come first, then develop advantages based on those values.*

3. *If advantages come first, then build values around those advantages.*

4. *Whichever is stronger in your organization, values or advantages, use the stronger one to influence the other.*

5. *If your organization possesses neither strong values nor strong advantages, you must begin working immediately to develop one or the other as a first step.*

6. *No matter how strong your current values or advantages, they will grow even stronger if they match one another.*

Applying Right Answers

"The teachers just don't seem to listen," complained a professor of education at a major university (I'll call her Gwenn). Gwenn and her husband, also a Ph.D. holder, were deeply concerned about the quality of education their two young children, a boy and a girl ages 6 and 8, were getting, but their children's teachers had not welcomed the Gwenn's "intrusion." Hoping to find some support, Gwenn became actively involved in the local PTA, where she met other parents who shared her frustration over a lack of communication with their children's teachers. Gwenn decided to act, taking a sabbatical from her university post for the purpose of establishing a private elementary and middle school providing superior education, based on her belief that parents should be encouraged to get anxiously involved.

After a year of arranging funding, finding a headmaster, and putting a faculty together, along with marketing the new idea to parents in the community, Gwenn was ready to go back to her university post and immerse herself in her research and teaching. Her dream thrived as the school established a compelling advantage in the marketplace, compared to other public and private schools. During the first year, the school reached its maximum capacity and began a long waiting list. The school's basic advantage of actively involving parents in their children's education attracted faculty who wanted to be part of providing a more comprehensive, complete educational experience for students.

After the first year of operation, the school, now a viable business endeavor, went after additional funding for expansion. As chairman of the board, Gwenn watched as the school, faculty, and staff developed additional supporting values around the one basic advantage she had instilled in the school. Eventually, what began as one strong advantage in the marketplace over time grew into a complete set of educational values that created new advantages. "One fed the other," Gwenn said recently. "Our advantage drew talented people, and those talented people developed additional important values that led to greater advantages."

The story has an even greater moral. The school's advantages and values became so strong, other public and private schools in the area began borrowing freely from its example. In this way, Gwenn's influence extended itself far beyond her own children and her own school's students.

18

Can You Sustain Your Advantages?

&

Many years ago, as kids in elementary school, we used to play tetherball at recess. With a lot of practice, I actually got pretty good at the game. I can still remember beating one particular opponent over and over again. I wondered why he kept playing and why he kept wanting to play with me. Even though I beat him every time, he just kept coming back for more. After the school year ended, I didn't see him for the whole summer, but when classes resumed again in the fall, I will never forget how this kid grabbed me in the hall at school and said, "I'll play you a game of tetherball at recess." I agreed, thinking that I'd just whip him again. Imagine my shock when he beat me soundly. How had he gotten so good, I wanted to know? "I've been practicing," he said. That experience continues to stay with me as a great example of why no one should ever expect advantages, whether personal or corporate, to remain constant over time. Sometimes, even a kid knows better than that.

Five years ago, then 19-year-old Michael Dell, not much more than a kid, decided to start a business. He knew a lot about computers, having practically grown up in the computer stores in the Houston area, so he surprised no one when he began selling IBM-PC clones directly to individuals and businesses from a University of Texas dormitory room. Using direct-response advertising and telemarketing techniques, the fledgling Dell Computer generated an impossible amount of business in a very short period of time. Eventually, the company added a direct sales force to sell its products around the world.

Dell Computer's major competitive advantage derived from its selling method, which put machines in the hands of its customers at a substantial savings over other retailers, who tacked hefty retailing markups on their products. Dell also provided solid after-sale service. As a result of its competitive advantages, Dell became a $70 million company in just three years. Michael Dell won all kinds of adulation and praise as a business "whiz-kid." *INC.* magazine honored him as an Entrepreneur of the Year in 1990.

ஐ *The Key Question*

How can you maintain and enhance your organization's competitive advantage(s) over time?

Dell Computer's Answer

After three years of effectively sustaining its sales and service advantages, Dell Computer began to encounter increasing competition and changing customer needs. Competitors began copying Dell's approach, and the marketplace steadily differentiated itself into distinct customer segments. It didn't take Michael Dell long to determine that he would eventually need to overhaul his company's sales and distribution advantage. Of course, the company's direct sales and distribution approach could continue as an integral part of its strategy, but to continue strong growth in the future, it would need to augment or replace its initial competitive advantages. With his usual imagination, Michael Dell decided to stop selling IBM PCs and clones and begin designing, producing, and selling his own PCs for a target market segment of relatively sophisticated users. The switchover has challenged the company, and recent departures of key executives indicate that it will not solve its problems easily. Perhaps Dell underestimated the importance of his organization's initial original competitive advantage and overestimated its ability to develop new ones quickly.

Suggested Right Answers

Sustained competitive advantage depends on taking a few basic steps:

1. *Monitor the exact status of your organization's competitive advantages at all times.*

2. *Regardless of your method of monitoring competitive advantage, keep a sharp eye open for even the subtlest changes in company operations, customer needs, competitor strategies, industry characteristics, government regulations, or other external environmental factors that may affect your organization's competitive advantages.*

3. *Before you attempt to develop a new competitive advantage, work to revitalize existing or old ones; it's cheaper and more effective.*

4. *Listen to suggestions from people in your organization regarding new ways to sustain, enhance, and/or replace, if absolutely necessary, existing advantages.*

Applying Right Answers

The director of management development at a large pharmaceutical company headquartered in the Midwest (I'll call him John) was becoming more and more concerned about a subtle trend within his company's R&D division toward increased structure and systemization. Although the firm's scientists seemed to be handling the organizational and operational changes gracefully, John's discomfort continued to grow. The pharmaceutical company enjoyed a deserved reputation for innovation and new product development, and almost everyone in the company would cite the company's ability to develop new products as its primary competitive advantage. Protecting that advantage preoccupied every executive and manager, especially when it came to strategic planning. As a result, the firm's vital competitive advantage seemed unshakable.

John, however, who shouldered responsibility for management development and training, thought he saw a potential threat to his company's innovation advantage. Since John worked every day grooming managers throughout the company, he had become acutely aware of the fact that the company's growth had resulted in an increasing bureaucratization that all large firms seem fated to suffer. Of course, this phenomenon would scarcely surprise or worry most executives and managers in a sprawling organization, who accept bureaucracy as an unpleasant but necessary byproduct of size and would just try hard to keep red tape to a minimum. Not John. He felt strongly that the expanding bureaucracy was already beginning to damage the creative freedom and flexible autonomy of the R&D division. Although scientists weren't complaining about it much, John argued that they wouldn't grumble until it was too late to do anything about it and the company's innovative advantage had eroded. "Scientists just don't pay attention to the subtle encroachments of structure and systems until it severely impairs them," John insisted. "We've got to act on this issue now!"

Because of John's persistent attention to sustaining the company's most important competitive advantage, the company has in fact taken steps to keep the R&D division free from as much bureaucratization as possible. John himself continually monitors the R&D

environment to ensure that no burdensome forms or reports or meetings be allowed to compromise the creativity and productivity of the company's scientists. As a result, the firm has been able to sustain its new product development advantage despite ferocious competition from its rivals in the industry.

19

Does Everyone Work to Sustain Your Advantages?

ক

*I*n football, your team's advantage depends on all the players pulling together. I recently watched with interest as two passing powerhouses clashed on the field. The pre-game analysts had identified pass defense as the single biggest element in the game's outcome, and one of the teams enjoyed a stronger reputation in that area, particularly with its deep backs. The four defensive backs on this team worked together as a unit, making it nearly impossible for an opposing quarterback to complete any pass beyond five yards. In the big game, they managed to shut down the long ball passing game for almost a quarter, but then, one of the defensive backs sustained an injury and had to be taken off the field on a stretcher. When the substitute proved not nearly as talented, the opposing team found a weakness. Passing again and again to the defense's weak spot, the opponent eventually won the game. Leaving the stadium, I pondered how critical it had been for that set of four deep defensive backs to work together to create a sustained advantage, and about how the same applies to organizations. If just one person falters and doesn't work to maintain and improve the organization's advantages, the resulting weakness can make the organization dangerously vulnerable.

Eastman Kodak has recently done a lot of work to make sure that everyone in its organization works diligently to sustain advantages. To accomplish this, the company implemented what it calls the "demassification" solution. Demassification means breaking down complex and large entities into smaller units that can function autonomously to move the organization forward, generating profit and securing advantage. This has meant creating small entrepreneurial plants, reducing corporate staffs and layers of management, decentralizing the management information system, and establishing computer networking. All this aims at the simple objective of enabling everyone in the organization to be more responsive to company challenges and more productive in applying competitive advantages for profit.

One example of demassification can be found in the firm's precision components manufacturing division, where assembly workers now arrange their own hours, keep track of and improve their productivity with their own suggestions, interview prospective recruits, and help manage "just in time" inventory. These measures will, the company hopes, help sustain cost and technology advantages in its various divisions.

❧ *The Key Question*

What, specifically, can you do to help every employee become more effective in maintaining or building the organization's competitive advantages?

Eastman Kodak's Answer

At Kodak's injection molding camera body division, the company subdivided the manufacturing plant into small, independent shops able to function on their own as suppliers and servicers for other units within the company. Since each unit now enjoys the autonomy to make decisions that effect its own profit, a given unit can, if it chooses, buy from vendors outside the company instead of from sister units. This autonomy also applies to each individual worker. As a result, people working in the division feel a responsibility to build their unit's advantages and make it the vendor of choice for other Kodak units. Preliminary results show Kodak's injection molding camera body division beginning to realize reduced inventory, increased worker productivity, decreased cost of information processing, and greatly improved inventory accuracy. In addition to all of these internal advantages, the division's ability to service customers has also increased dramatically. This means a lot to the Eastman Kodak Company as a whole because many of this division's customers are other divisions of Eastman Kodak.

Suggested Right Answers

Every employee in an organization should sustain that organization's competitive advantages. In order to achieve maximum individual effectiveness, you can do the following:

1. *Create the right environment through demassification, decentralization, or right-sizing.*

2. *Make sure every employee appreciates the organization's competitive advantages.*

3. *Give every employee the opportunity to track his or her own performance in terms of maintaining or building advantages.*

4. *Award your people the autonomy to sustain advantages.*

5. *When autonomy begins to work against your ability to coordinate and orchestrate, give your people more responsibility for solving that problem.*

6. *Use the notion of competitive advantage to tie together issues of customer service, quality, cost, and productivity.*

7. *Recognize that the concept of competitive advantage is just as powerful for an individual as it is for the organization as a whole.*

8. *Don't forget that only your people can create new competitive advantages.*

Applying Right Answers

At a large consumer products company that manufactures a lot of different snack foods, I've seen considerable attention paid to new product development. The ability to come up with new kinds of snack foods plays such a key role in this company's long-term success that it encourages everyone in the organization to get involved in the process. The secretary to the vice president of brand marketing (I'll call her Margaret) has been with the company for more than 20 years. Margaret does more than just type and take dictation, however. Fully aware of the company's need to sustain its competitive advantage in new product development and introduction, Margaret develops recipes at home for sauces, dips, and seasonings. No one asked her to do this; she simply does it because of her own clear understanding of what new product development means to the company and because of her own interest in cooking and experimenting with new tastes. A few years ago, in recognition of Margaret's efforts, the company began to give Margaret bonus checks for any innovations that became part of a new snack food, dip, or sauce. The reward has made Margaret grateful for the company's recognition of her talent, but as she says, "I don't expect to get paid for what I do beyond my job as a secretary, because I feel it is my responsibility as an employee of this company to try to help it do its job better and become the most successful company it can become. I'm really no different from anyone else around here, because we are all aware of what this company needs to do to succeed."

Margaret's words tell us a lot about this company. Given the fact that people like her are acutely aware of exactly what the organization is trying to accomplish and what advantages it must sustain, the company enjoys the most important advantage of all.

20

Are Your Advantages Paying Off?

— ❧ —

A few years ago, when we were selling our house, we decided to finish off the basement, because we thought that would give us an advantage in the marketplace. Over the next several months, we discovered that having a finished basement wasn't an advantage at all, as potential buyers either complained that they didn't want to pay for a finished basement or that they wanted to finish off their own basement. Although we clearly did create an advantage over other homes in the neighborhood, that advantage didn't do us much good. In the end, it ended up costing us money. It's no surprise that organizations do the same thing, spending a lot of money to develop an advantage that accomplishes little or nothing in the way of return or profit.

Blue Bell Creameries is an ice cream company headquartered 70 miles north of Houston. It owns 60 percent of the ice cream market in Texas and maintains several competitive advantages, including a down-home image, higher-quality ingredients for the price, a store-door delivery system, and a high market share track record. At $160 million per year, it ranked as the second biggest brand after Kraft General Foods's Breyer's brand in the country. Blue Bell executives, knowing they were doing about as much business as they could possibly hope to do in the state of Texas, decided to try to move across the state line and enter nearby markets. Like a lot of small- to medium-size local companies that reach a saturation point in their own markets, Blue Bell had little other choice for growth. The question facing Blue Bell: Could the advantages that played so well in Texas position them in markets where customers did not know about Blue Bell ice cream?

⋟ *The Key Question*

Do your competitive advantages really pay off in terms of higher margins, growth opportunities, customer loyalty, or any other performance measures?

Blue Bell's Answer

The people at Blue Bell, led by chairman and CEO Edward Kruse, moved into the Oklahoma City and New Orleans markets. Attempting to capitalize upon and communicate each of its key advantages, the company sent out information to radio and television stations in the new markets about Blue Bell's small town beginnings, along with free samples of its product. It spent a lot of money on advertising the high quality of its ice cream at a reasonable price, and it put its store-door distribution system into action, visiting the stores on a daily basis to make sure they were well stocked and satisfied.

The great success of Blue Bell in the Texas market helped salesmen convince stores in New Orleans and Oklahoma City that they would see greater product turnover with Blue Bell than with current products. Within three months, Blue Bell achieved over 35 percent market share in New Orleans. It took a little longer in the Oklahoma City market because there it competed against an entrenched local brand. Still, over a 10-month period, Blue Bell achieved a 33 percent share of the market. In each of the two markets, Blue Bell ice cream became the largest single ice cream seller in grocery stores.

Blue Bell's advantages turned out to be real, and they paid off handsomely. Not only have the Blue Bell advantages provided opportunities for the firm to move into new markets, they have also consistently produced margins 50 to 100 percent higher than those of other regional dairy companies around the country. Wherever you live, you, too, may be eating Blue Bell ice cream soon.

Suggested Right Answers

When evaluating your own competitive advantages, you should think about the following:

1. *Remember that you can and should test every competitive advantage to determine whether it pays off.*

2. *Never refer to any difference or uniqueness as a competitive advantage if it is not paying off in terms of specific tangible or intangible results.*

3. *If a real and tested competitive advantage is paying off, increase the results you are obtaining from it by further exploiting it.*

Applying Right Answers

It's not unusual for a company to get so wrapped up in an internalized view of its competitive advantages that it fails to evaluate its advantages in terms of bottom-line results. This happened at a division of a large retailing company that was experiencing mediocre results and yet continued to claim superior advantages in the marketplace. At one point, the newly appointed division president (I'll call her Liz), was asked by senior executives of the parent company to find out what was really going on in the company and to get it back on track. The division consisted of a chain of upscale women's clothing stores that enjoyed an unusually high level of unity and self-esteem among executives, managers, and employees throughout the chain. This contributed a valuable "esprit de corps" to the division, but, as Liz found out, it also caused people to view their competitive advantages through rose-colored glasses.

Liz dug in immediately, trying to find out exactly why margins and profit levels had sagged. Everyone she talked to boasted that the chain carried the highest-quality women's clothing in the markets it served, and it delivered unequaled customer service. However, Liz's experience told her that if the chain really did deliver superior quality and service, it should be recording higher margins and greater profits for the division. Liz considered that since the perceived advantages were not paying off, perhaps the stores were mismatched with their markets and customers. However, based on her experience in the retailing business and her first-hand knowledge of the markets where her division's stores operated, she concluded that a large demand for high quality and superior service should exist. Therefore, the problem lay elsewhere.

Liz proceeded to oversee a number of customer surveys and market analyses as well as internal assessments of the division's results. Since she expected to find that the advantages so valiantly claimed within the division by employees and managers were not as strong as everyone thought, she was surprised to find out that customers really did recognize these advantages and did choose to shop at the chain's stores because of them. In fact, the data was so overwhelming that Liz used it to move the company into a new position. At a two-day retreat for the senior executives of the division, she presented the data and then unfolded a new plan: "We have these advantages, so we can and should raise prices to maintain acceptable profits." Although many voiced strong resistance to Liz's plan, arguing that "higher prices would drive customers away," and "the competition will eat us alive," Liz held fast to her position and over the next six months raised prices an average of 10 to 15% across the board. This move would prove the acid test for the division's competitive advantages. It took only a few months to prove that customer loyalty continued with sales increasing in dollar volume by the price percentage increases. In the end, the advantages that this division touted turned out to be real advantages that could have been paying off all along. During the following two years, Liz's division reported earnings above the industry average.

Part V

TALENT

❧

21

Do You Recognize Your Own Genius?

━━━━━━━━━━ ‌𞸑 ━━━━━━━━━━

Genius is a funny word. Somehow we tend to associate it with towering intellect, an Albert Einstein or a Carl Jung or even a Henry Ford. But I've come to realize after years of working with business people that each of us has at least a dash of his or her own genius. Look at the character Kevin Costner played in the movie *Dances with Wolves*, a fellow unable to cope with the requirements of war but with a pure genius for stripping away the foolish preoccupations and mindless prejudices that plague so many in this life. I related to that character, as so many movie-goers did, because he, like so many of us, just took his genius for granted. It was just *him*, it came effortlessly, so he tended to devalue it.

I was especially struck by this notion when I looked into the surprising turnaround of Harley-Davidson. After virtually inventing the biker image, the company lost its market to sleeker, less expensive, more reliable machines from Japan. By the early 1980s, the company was losing millions of dollars a year as its market share skidded from 75 percent to below 25 percent. Though the company seemed perched on the brink of demise, management leveraged it out from its parent AMF and began the daunting task of beating the Japanese competition. Enter a genius, in the form of one William G. Davidson, grandson of a company founder and vice president of styling. A biker at heart, with his beard and black leather garb, Willie G., as he likes to be called, may not have looked like a Wall Street turnaround specialist, but he was attuned, in every molecule of his being, to the needs and desires of a generation of motorcyclists devoted to their "Harleys." Being raised as a Davidson certainly explains part of his interest in motorcycles, but it goes much deeper than that. According to Willie G. himself, he is "obsessed" with the look, feel, and symbol of the Harley-Davidson motorcycle and that obsession includes understanding and personifying the bikers who own them. More than a corporate representative, Willie G. is first and foremost the biker's representative with an unusual gift for sensing and envisioning accoutrements that keep the Harley devotees, past and present, loyal.

Because so much of a motorcycle is exposed, the styling of the machine, from instrumentation to engine, pipes, wheels, and seats, makes a big difference to bikers who know exactly what they like and don't like. Willie G., sharing those likes and dislikes, brought his styling genius to bear and bought the company the credibility and time it needed to kick-start the turnaround. He had a genius for styling a motorcycle's looks, components, and accessories, and that genius, more than anything else, accounts for one of the most heralded corporate comebacks in business history. After a five-year effort, manufacturing substance followed artistic style, and once again "made in America" motorcycles were thundering down the highway. Harley-Davidson went on in the next few years to recapture much of its lost prestige, gaining a full 50 percent of the market and restoring profits to its financial performance.

❧ The Key Question

How can you make sure your organization takes full advantage of your genius?

Harley-Davidson's Answer

Willie G. didn't develop and pursue his own unique genius just because he thought one day that he might be able to save his grandfather's company. Rather, he did what he loved most in the world. It was a simple case of the old saying, "Do what you love, the money will follow." If you do what you love, you'll work hard at it and get better and better at it. Willie G. had been sharpening his genius within the company all along, but not until a few years ago did it place him center stage. That's the way it is with most of us. If we work hard to find and develop our genius, there will come special times in our professional and personal lives when the time, effort, and concentration can move us to center stage. At Harley-Davidson, the drama revolved around a crisis. In our own undertakings, it may involve a start-up, an innovation, a merger, an investment, a reorganization or even a career change, but no matter what the plot, the success of the play will hinge on the genius of the author.

Suggested Right Answers

The following points can help guide your personal and organizational quests to find and apply your genius:

1. *Genius comes in many, often undramatic, forms. Never sell yourself short, but constantly search for and define your own unique talent.*

2. *Once you recognize your real genius and can clearly describe it, find an organizational or working environment that needs and will nurture it.*

3. *With an understanding of your genius and the right match between it and your work, continue to develop and apply your genius with patience and dedication.*

4. Keep an eye out for those critical situations when your genius can flourish.

Applying Right Answers

Sometimes it takes a while to find your real genius, and when you do finally discover it, you may realize that your present environment doesn't adequately tap it. If so, you'll probably need to make a change. A Harvard MBA (I'll call him Bill) graduated in the top 10 percent of his class and was intent on a career in marketing. He joined a well-known consumer products company's product marketing group and over the next six years, Bill worked hard but never really felt challenged or excited by his job. Oh, he undertook some important assignments and did some good things, but overall he began to feel that he had not done much to live up to his graduate school promise. Through it all, Bill found that his love for product marketing had gradually waned. In fact, he began wondering why marketing had ever lured him in the first place.

To his credit, Bill finally engaged in some soul searching in an effort to determine what he really wanted out of his life and career. That probing brought him to what, in retrospect, seemed a too-obvious conclusion: In his present job he hadn't gotten enough contact with people out in the marketplace. In school, it had been his interaction with people that had won him distinction. While he seldom completed a quantitative course with honors, he excelled in any discussion where qualitative issues were concerned. His classmates thought of him as a "people" person. Although he had been interacting with people in the company for the past six years, he now found himself yearning for more. All the time he spent analyzing product positions, product strategies, and product test markets would always, it seemed, get in the way of that goal.

Before long, Bill left the company and made a fairly major career adjustment, joining a large investment banking firm on the West Coast as a stockbroker. Bill had decided that he could become a great stockbroker because success would depend a great deal on his people skills with colleagues, analysts, and clients. In the new firm, Bill had to start at the bottom of the ladder, competing with younger people who had just joined the firm, but his genius for getting along with and winning the confidence of a broad assortment of people helped him over the awkward initial stages of his new career. Skills from his old job, especially his knowledge of positioning products and judging the successes of companies and products, also served him well.

In the years that followed, Bill rose through the ranks quite quickly, proving that he had found the right environment for his genius to flourish. Colleagues respected him, and his clients came to value his understanding of their needs. He was particularly brilliant at matching the desires of his clients with particular, often unusual, investment packages. Within five years, he became the most successful of his office's 200 brokers. If you ask him if he's happy now, he'll most likely wink and say, "I almost outsmarted myself after Harvard. I thought my genius was dumb, but oh, was *that* dumb!"

22

Do You Fully Appreciate Everyone's Talents?

───── ❧ ─────

*R*ecently, as chairman of a large youth conference, I had to select youngsters from a steering committee for key assignments such as taking care of the food and lodging, arranging the music and a dramatic production, dealing with finances, and a number of other responsibilities. Although I knew some of the 16 young people on the steering committee better than others, I felt quite confident I could make appropriate matches. After all, wasn't I a management consultant who specialized in assessing the talents and capabilities of people?

You can imagine my surprise when, the minute I communicated assignments to the steering committee, many expressed dismay, and I soon had a small mutiny on my hands. As I listened to their complaints, I realized that I had really done very little to match assignments to individual talents, capabilities, and interests. When I let them allocate the responsibilities themselves, they did so beautifully. The conference was a huge success. The experience taught me a great lesson about understanding and applying people's talents.

As chairman and CEO of General Electric Company, with revenues of over $60 billion, Jack Welch has streamlined and simplified a massive organization, in the process creating a model many other organizations will follow in the decade ahead. Welch argues that most organizations place too much emphasis on control, bureaucracy, and complex management systems. He believes we need the speed, simplicity, and self-confidence you can get by giving people the opportunity to dream, risk, and revolutionize. If you've ever heard Jack Welch speak, you probably listened to his plea for embracing vision and passion, and eliminating management systems that overcontrol and overcomplicate most organizations. To his mind, America's competitive advantage lies in the irreverence, aggressiveness, impatience, and curiosity of its people, traits that should form the core of organizational cultures because they allow people to move quickly, develop passionate visions, and break new ground. In some ways, Welch sounds almost like an evangelist, preaching the doom and gloom that will come if we don't bring leadership to bear on our organizations.

❧ *The Key Question*

How do you make sure that you fully value everyone's talents?

Jack Welch's Answer

According to Jack Welch, there is no room for "managers" in the best organizations of the future. In other words, anyone whose talents make them practical, reasonable, decisive, orderly, systematic, or controlled will serve little purpose in the decade ahead. Welch's message to such people is simple: Develop leadership talents or find work elsewhere.

What do you think about Jack Welch's vision of the future? Is he right or has he overly narrowed his position? To my way of thinking, the best organizations benefit from a full array of talents, which includes the ability to "manage" in the traditional sense of the word. However, in all fairness to Jack Welch, he has been working hard to transform a management-dominated bureaucracy into an agile and flexible giant that can dance. In so doing, he has overemphasized the role of creative, visionary leadership because it has been suppressed or ignored in environments like GE's in the past. Jack is simply valuing talents that are not only extremely important in today's business environment, but ones that have been undervalued in recent years among large corporations.

Suggested Right Answers

When assessing and valuing talents to build stronger cultures, consider the following points:

1. *Value both leaders and managers, both the conceptual and the practical, both the flexible and the decisive, both the feeling and the thinking, and so on.*

2. *Rather than pitting opposites or differences against one another, try to apply each to the right assignments and opportunities.*

3. *Don't expect people to change their inherent characteristics and qualities; rather exploit and further develop the innate strengths in people.*

4. *Ultimately, the strongest organizational cultures enjoy the greatest diversity of talents and capabilities.*

Applying Right Answers

The retired CEO of a large division of a major U.S. corporation (I'll call him Richard), recently wrote an editorial article for the business section of a large metropolitan newspaper in which he expressed how he felt "demeaned by the recent hoopla about leadership." He bemoaned the fact that an overemphasis on leadership or any set of capabilities or skills prevents executives from fully understanding and applying "the amazing variety of gifts individuals bring to their jobs."

At one point in his article, he used a simple analogy: "I know it sounds trite, but a tribe needs Indians as well as chiefs, cooks as well as hunters, storytellers as well as bowmakers. Why can't we respect what each person can uniquely contribute?"

To drive home his point, Richard described a situation in his business career where his boss had concluded that Richard did not have the necessary talents to succeed in business. The boss was quite frank: "Either develop leadership capabilities or do something else with your life." That advice left Richard feeling distraught and confused, and wondering how he could develop the talents his boss deemed so critical.

In the weeks and months that followed, Richard labored desperately to comprehend what his boss wanted him to do and be, but when he eventually concluded that he just couldn't please the man, he chose to leave the company and join another. In 10 years, he became CEO of the new firm's largest division. Looking back from his retirement years, Richard felt the experience taught him the importance of diverse talents in an organization. "How boring—and unproductive—it would be if we stamped every worker out of the same mold—even if it is a beautiful mold."

23

Can You Find New Ways to Apply Existing Talents?

━━━━━━━━━━ ࣾ ━━━━━━━━━━

*A*merican business people tend to identify new opportunities in the marketplace and then hire the appropriate talent to seize those opportunities. The Japanese, on the other hand, will most likely examine their skills and talents, then look outside to see how they can take advantage of opportunities by applying those talents in new ways. This difference in orientation played itself out during a brainstorming session with a mixed group of American and Japanese business people. The group wanted to discover new ways to apply the capabilities and talents that existed within a major joint venturing project. By the end of our brainstorming session, the Japanese participants had contributed five to one over the Americans in terms of new viable possibilities for applying existing capabilities and talents in new markets. This experience was one more evidence that the Japanese have been so successful in recent years because they are so good at finding new ways to apply the existing expertise, capabilities, and talents of their people and organizations. Of course, some Americans know how to do it, too.

When George Shinn became the owner of the NBA's most recent franchise, the Charlotte Hornets, he faced two big problems: First, Charlotte represents the second-smallest market among the

NBA's 27 teams; second, when you launch a new franchise, you must build your team largely with castoffs from other franchises. Thus, George Shinn entered his first season in 1988 to 1989 with talent that had never worked together before and would not likely turn a profit for several years. Not content with this situation, George Shinn set about finding a way to apply the talents of his club in new ways. Although he knew his team would suffer through some losing seasons during the first few years, he was determined to speed things up. So he started examining everything about the team, the players, the staff, the management, and the community.

❧ The Key Question

Do you seriously strive to find new ways to apply existing talents?

The Hornets's Answer

Since George Shinn realized that his new team couldn't possibly be competitive from its inception, he refocused his managerial talent and that of his executive staff on every other possible customer service aspect of the team that he could control in order to make each game an enjoyable experience for every fan—even if the Hornets lost. Despite the team's handicaps as a brand-new franchise, why couldn't the Hornets provide top-flight service? Every franchise possesses the talent to serve its season ticket holders, but how could the Hornets do a better job? At George Shinn's urging, the club's general manager, Carl Sheer, instituted a five-step value system in terms of how to deal with season ticket holders. The values incorporated such ideas as "the season ticket holder is the most important person to us; we depend upon the season ticket holder, not the other way around; we should never think of the season ticket holder as interrupting the work that we have to get done; we should never argue with a season ticket holder; and we should do everything within our power to meet the wants and desires of every season ticket holder." While every franchise has to deal with season ticket holders, the Hornets began to make it their key focus, fine-tuning their marketing and managerial talent in ways that other franchises had never done before.

Managerially, the franchise also focused on simple items, such as providing suitable parking, making sure that restrooms were ultra-clean, arranging for spectacular half-time entertainment, and making the club a key component of the community.

Shinn got his athletic talent involved on the playing floor and also in the community, doing more than other teams' players in terms of local public service and charity work. He even got them to do small things, such as eliminating on-court swearing and participating in nondenominational invocations at the beginning of every game. As a result, the players felt an integral part of both the new franchise and the community.

George Shinn also worked hard to involve his management and atheletes in drawing the Charlotte community into the team's activities. A North Carolinian fashion designer created the team's uniforms. The team conducted community surveys to name the team and predict the team's draft picks. Every person who works for the club accepts responsibility for selling the team every day to civics clubs, rotary meetings, Y.M.C.A.s, community events, and neighborhood parties. In its first season, the Charlotte Hornets lost 62 of their 82 games, but they set records for attendance, averaging 23,000 fans per home game, 1500 fans more than the NBA's second place Detroit franchise. The team not only enjoys tremendous support from the community, it turned a larger profit in the 1989–1990 season than any NBA team—$11 million. Other NBA teams may boast greater talents than the Charlotte Hornets, but George Shinn's people apply their talents like no other team in the league.

Suggested Right Answers

*Whenever you find yourself looking for new ways to apply
the current talents within your organization, remember:*

1. *Every organization wastes the talents of its people in one way
   or another.*

2. *Most people need help in finding new ways to apply their
   talents.*

3. *You can **always** find better ways to apply people's talents.*

Applying Right Answers

A medical products firm headquartered on the West Coast had
stagnated for a few years in terms of product development. Several years earlier, the company had introduced a revolutionary
patient oxygen system that had allowed the company to grow in
excess of $200 million in sales per year. But since that major in-
novation, the company's R&D had attained little success.

In an effort to remedy the situation, the company had hired someone (I'll call him Paul) from another part of the parent organization
to assume the reins of director of R&D, reporting to the executive
vice president of the company. Well aware of the challenge facing
him, Paul decided to assess the engineering and scientific talent
of the R&D group before trying any changes. During his review,
Paul discovered a brilliant engineer (I'll call him Harry) five years
away from retirement, yet extremely frustrated with what had
been happening within the company over the last several years.
Clearly, Harry's talent had not been effectively applied in recent
years. Harry himself had devised the original oxygen system that
accounted for over $100 million in revenue for the company each
year, but his efforts over the seven years since that breakthrough
had produced little more than wheel spinning. As Paul probed
into the history of the initial invention, he discovered that the

company's former president had charged Harry to find a better way to get oxygen to acute care patients at a price that most community hospitals could afford. He rose to that challenge. After that, however, Harry could not effectively chart his own course or come up with his own notion of a new product. Soon after that first system had come to market, the company president had moved up to corporate headquarters, leaving Harry to his own devices.

Since Paul possessed a mixture of engineering and marketing skills, he could imagine potential products Harry might create. As soon as Paul gave Harry clear direction, identifying three specific areas that appeared most promising, Harry got to work with renewed vigor. Eighteen months later, Harry had developed three new prototypes that eventually became dominant new products for the company. Harry's talents just needed to be redirected and reapplied, and luckily or wisely, Paul looked for new ways to stimulate this award-winning veteran.

24

Are You Maximizing Talents?

───── ❧ ─────

A number of television specials in recent months have depicted the plight of our public school systems. One of these profiled two schools in different communities with different economic bases. The dollars spent per student in one community was about $2500, in the other over $10,000. The program singled out a few similar students from each school, interviewing them in an effort to compare results. Sadly but predictably, two eighth-graders from each school, while both bright, interested in becoming writers, and at the head of their classes, showed dramatically different results. The child in the well-funded program had already published five short stories, several poems, and was working on a novel. The other student had yet to publish a single word. As these two students talked about their futures, the successes that the one had already achieved clearly fueled his dreams, while the other student hesitated, wondering whether he would ever publish anything. What a difference it makes in people's lives when they feel their talents are being maximized!

Thermo Electron Corporation, a highly successful $600 million company headquartered in Waltham, Massachusetts, develops and manufactures biomedical, process control, environmental, instrumentation, and power-generation products. Spread out over 17 locations in the United States and Canada, the United Kingdom, France, Japan, West Germany, Holland, and Hong Kong, the firm also provides services in such areas as metallurgical heat-treating, water quality engineering, analytical laboratory work, and contract research and development.

A few years ago, the company began breaking itself up into smaller independent subsidiaries, with Thermo Electron retaining the majority shareholder interest in each unit that went public. Now investors could buy stock in the parent or any daughter company, and employees of the company and its subsidiaries could garner generous stock options based on their performance. As a result, a steady stream of successful, innovative products and services, ranging from a battery-powered human heart-assist device to an industrial electricity cogeneration system have helped the organization to a level of performance nothing short of remarkable.

According to George Hatsopoulos, founder and CEO of Thermo Electron, effective application of the many different capabilities of his company's people accounts for its success. To his mind, three overriding concerns help maximize talents within Thermo Electron: 1) a broad strategic focus on mechanical engineering, 2) a corporate culture that promotes creative thinking, and 3) a strong commitment to risk taking. Such focus, creativity, and commitment help keep individual effectiveness running like a stream throughout the organization. Amazingly, during the company's 33-year history, no employee has left to start a rival business.

❧ The Key Question

What does it take to maximize the talents of the people in your organization?

Thermo Electron's Answer

George Hatsopoulos believes in the marriage of large and small, freedom and performance, innovation and results. His initial concept of the company, which he started after graduating from M.I.T. with a doctoral degree, entailed working on numerous, potentially profitable mechanical engineering ideas simultaneously. That notion still guides the company today. While the parent organization provides the stability and size advantages of a large firm with adaptable accounting, personnel, and marketing services, the daughter companies supply the innovation, vision, and flexibility to keep Thermo Electron thriving. Not only does this environment harness a wide range of talents, it allows investors, who Hatsopoulos believes can better judge risk return, potential, and profit than corporate line managers, to become key stakeholders in the firm's performance.

Although no set rules govern project or idea funding, every undertaking must display big payoff potential. Part of the secret behind Thermo Electron's success lies in the way talented individuals enjoy the freedom to pursue ideas. For instance, one engineer began working on an air pollution instrument that eventually led to blood gas analysis equipment and a bomb-detection device. This example illustrates a crucial point: Within a clear structure (mechanical engineering), people with diverse talents (metallurgy, thermodynamics, fluids, and other specializations) can freely drive toward innovation and results. Thermo Electron has simplified the start-up and subsidiary creation process to maximize the incentives and payoffs whenever a project becomes hot.

Suggested Right Answers

*Five keys can unlock the talents of the people
in your organization:*

1. *Create and maintain an environment that fosters a broad spectrum of perspectives, even the most conflicting ones.*

2. *Communicate openly about differences of opinion and viewpoint, encouraging others to do likewise.*

3. *Revamp people-development programs, constantly tailoring them to unique individuals.*

4. *Make sure you are maximizing your own unique talents and abilities.*

5. *Work hard to value and appreciate the unique talents and abilities of others as much as your own (or your own as much as others').*

Applying Right Answers

A graduate from Stanford with an MBA in marketing (I'll call him Sam) went to work for Procter & Gamble as an assistant brand manager in the bar soap product group. He stayed with the company for five years, attaining the rank of brand manager before he accepted a position with a small, family-owned tea and hot drink mix company in his home town. His new employer, the son of the firm's founder, having decided it was time to implement a more sophisticated and professional marketing approach, had hired Sam as his first Marketing vice president.

However, after two years of struggling to infuse cutting-edge marketing techniques into the firm, Sam felt like throwing in the towel. Despite Herculean efforts on his part, not one significant change had occurred, at least from his beleaguered viewpoint. He once complained, "I've tried everything I can think of to get this company to adopt the most rudimentary marketing approaches, but no one sees the need; they just treat me as a stuffy corporate type who's trying to take all the fun out of working here." Sam lamented most bitterly that his own talents were going to waste and might even atrophy in such an environment.

As a last attempt to salvage something from his two-year stint, Sam met away from the office with the company's president (I'll call him Bud). Without preamble, Sam vented his frustrations and told Bud he was looking for another job. Genuinely surprised, Bud asked his unhappy vice president why he hadn't come to him earlier. To Sam's amazement, Bud went on to cite his own frustrations with Sam's lack of progress. "In fact," Bud stated bluntly, "I've been thinking about letting you go." As the two men explored the situation together, it became clear that Bud had inadvertently sabotaged some of Sam's efforts by telling his other officers and managers not to worry about massive marketing changes because "we don't have to revolutionize this company overnight." Unfortunately, this stance, designed to ease Sam into the organization, backfired by giving people a justification for their disregard of "the new marketing kid's" programs. For his part, Sam could see that he had not taken sufficient care to put people's minds at ease, especially older employees who feared Sam might replace them with young hotshots.

Both men came to appreciate that the whole problem revolved around maximizing talents, not just Sam's, but the whole organization's. Bud agreed to set the record straight in terms of his own commitment to improve and professionalize the company's marketing activities, and Sam agreed to design a marketing fundamentals training course for all the company's officers and managers. The two men would convene every two weeks to monitor progress on both fronts. As it turned out, Sam stayed with the company and eventually helped it develop a marketing system that produced a sales increase from $18 million to over $40 million in 18 months. Sam was finally maximizing his talent and by so doing helped others maximize their talents. Effectiveness soared throughout the entire organization.

25

Do You Have the Right Talents to Succeed?

ಎ

Does this story sound familiar? A bright and promising MBA left after graduation to join a reputable international management consulting firm. Given the intense competition for the few slots at that firm, many of his classmates envied the fellow. Over the years, however, it became clear that he lacked some of the right skills needed to succeed in the consulting game. When, five years out of business school, his firm fired him, he was crushed. As he searched his soul, trying to figure out what he was going to do with his professional life, he turned to one of his former business school professors for guidance, and that proved to be just the ticket. The professor helped him recognize that he was simply suffering from a misalignment of his talents and could readily apply his real talents to the right undertaking.

After undergoing an array of self-assessment exercises, he spotted the right career track, and, sure enough, in the 10 years since that insight, he has done extremely well, currently serving as the division president of a $200 million company. The moral of that story about initially misdirected talents holds true for companies as well.

Donald Fisher, founder and CEO of The Gap, a chain of retailing outlets that capitalized on the jeans craze of the 1970s, built his company to a level of $500 million in sales. Fisher had seen a great market opportunity among teenagers and young adults and had capitalized on his own real estate experience and background to make his company work. His real estate experience allowed him to dot the country with his outlets, invariably positioning locations where they could flourish.

Before long, his empire included 550 stores, but even so, Fisher felt that something was missing. He dreamed of creating a company that could be perpetually successful, providing quality clothing to a broad range of customers, but he concluded that he himself lacked the necessary merchandising talent. Though he wisely turned to people within the company with strong retailing experience and talent, Fisher just couldn't find the right mix of talent in the early 1980s. Unwilling to shelve his vision, he began looking for that missing talent elsewhere.

❧ The Key Question

Can you identify the talents you need but currently lack?

The Gap's Answer

Don Fisher found his missing talent at rival retailer Ann Taylor. Millard Drexler, better known as Mickey, was working as president of Ann Taylor at the time Don Fisher made his offer. Drexler certainly possessed the kind of talent that The Gap needed, and he brought tremendously masterful merchandising to the company in 1983, transforming it from a teenage jeans and shirt focus to one that included classic and comfortable clothing for lmost everybody. And everyone at The Gap seems keenly intent upon maintaining its reputation for quality and style. Drexler's sense of what works and what doesn't work in retailing was exactly the right kind of talent The Gap needed to perpetuate its success.

The Gap has recently opened *Gap Kids*, which caters to children, and it will soon open *Baby Gap*. In the decade since the early 1980s, the company's sales have increased threefold to more than $1.5 billion, with profits jumping sixfold to more than $100 million. Yes, the company ran into a few problems along the way, especially with its ill-fated Banana Republic chain, but overall The Gap's bottom-line performance shines in the midst of so many mediocre and failing retailing companies today.

Suggested Right Answers

These guidelines will help you ensure that you've got the right talent in your organization to succeed:

1. *Always value existing talents fully, understanding, applying, and maximizing them to their fullest.*
2. *Openly discuss other talents you may need.*
3. *Acquire missing talents aggressively.*
4. *Work to blend new talents gracefully into the old.*

Applying Right Answers

The managing partner of a small professional services firm (I'll call him Max) had started the firm with two close associates, who together formed the executive committee for the firm. The three were very close friends, both professionally and socially. They had also participated together in many investments, so after 10 years their financial investments had become tightly interwoven.

Max lamented that only he among the three partners felt they lacked the talent necessary to build the firm beyond its current size of 30 professionals. The other fellows believed that among them existed the ability not only to continue building the firm but even to introduce it into adjacent markets. Max, on the other hand, thought growth would require merging with other firms and drawing additional people into the partnership. Max's two associates vehemently fought that notion.

What bothered Max most was that "my partners don't know what they don't know." After many often rancorous discussions with his partners, Max began to believe that maybe he was overreacting and they really could dredge up the ability to embark on a new phase of growth. Over the next year, Max's company opened offices in two new cities in the region. Although this strategy got the firm into two new markets, the attendant headaches were enormous. All of Max's worst fears resurfaced as the partnership sank hundreds of thousands of dollars into the management of the expanded firm. To make matters worse, three key individuals left to form their own organization because they despaired of ever getting into the partnership. Overnight, everything seemed to be going wrong. As the partners scrambled to put out an increasing number of fires, their preoccupation with internal problems became so evident that clients began wondering whether the firm could service their needs. Many defected to competitors.

Max met with his two associates in a number of grueling sessions during which they objectively examined each of their individual talents and constructed a list of missing ingredients. As they gradually agreed upon the missing talents, they began to sense the need to acquire them and provide a means for them to enter the partnership. Specifically, they decided to bring two additional people into the partnership, one with a strong marketing background and one with a brilliant track record in client relationships and servicing. A year later, the situation had improved dramatically, and Max expressed with a smile, "It's not what you don't know that hurts you, it's what you think you know that ain't so."

Part VI

MOTIVATION

26

What Strategic Priorities Motivate You Most?

— ❧ —

*E*arly in my business career I worked as a corporate staff analyst with a group vice president who had 21 divisions reporting to him. Nine of the divisions produced chemicals, 11 of them plastics. After sitting through numerous strategy sessions and providing various analyses for the group vice president, I concluded that he favored the plastics over the chemical companies. He seemed to like the fact that the plastics companies made tangible products, such as styrofoam cups, dinnerware, fasteners, containers, auto parts, electronic component casings, and even furniture. The chemical companies, on the other hand, just made chemicals, with less tangible form. I watched with interest during strategy sessions as the group VP would ask the senior executives of a plastics division to lay out some of their products on the table. He would look at them, touch them, and express great interest in them because they seemed to provide evidence of his accomplishments as an executive. I never saw him generate the same kind of excitement over chemical products. Not surprisingly, he fought harder to get capital expenditures approved for the plastics divisions, spent more time with them, and looked for additional acquisitions to augment the group, all the while treating the chemical companies with benign neglect. Over the years, the plastics divisions naturally became the dominant force, even though the chemical companies could have fared just as well under a different executive. That's when I first realized how big a role individual motivation can play in setting strategic priorities. You can see the proof every day in all sorts of companies.

Mrs. Fields Cookies, admired for its rapid growth throughout the 1980s, operates the red and white shops that have become familiar landmarks in shopping malls around the world. In 1987, Mrs. Fields opened 173 company-owned and operated stores, for a grand total of 543 worldwide. However, as the 1980s drew to an end, Debbie Fields, company president and founder, found herself spread way too thin as she tried to control everything herself: marketing, planning, operations, finance, etc. During this stage of development, her chain lost $19 million dollars, largely due to poor expansion planning. That forced Debbie Fields to question her strategic priorities.

After a lot of soul-searching, she kept returning to the fact that attention to customers' needs motivated her more than anything else, and that motivation lay behind her desire to stay close to the local managers who were also close to customers. Unfortunately, she had neglected these priorities while addressing all the other needs of the business.

✒ The Key Question

Do you link the personal motivations of people to the strategic priorities of the entire operation?

Mrs. Fields's Answer

While Debbie Fields recognized that her company must adhere to a number of strategic priorities, from operations to finance, in order to achieve success, she finally realized, too, that she could not pay proper attention to them all herself. Trying to do so had gotten her in trouble before, so she hired two new key executives to bolster her own talents. Tom Pierce, formerly with Price Waterhouse, became the chief financial officer, and Paul Baird, a former top executive with Godfather's Pizza, became head of operations. These two individuals followed their own personal motivations to set strategic priorities in operations and finance, and their coming aboard allowed Debbie to pursue her own main motivation and key strategic priority of customer needs and desires.

In her restricted role, she could spend time reviewing the hundreds of comments sent in every month by customers and participate in regular meetings with local store managers to discuss the needs of customers and how Mrs. Fields might expand into bakeries and other areas related to its core business. By 1990, profits had risen 17 percent over 1989, and the company seems likely to prosper in several avenues of growth, especially with bakeries. Debbie Fields plans to open about 250 of them before 1995.

Suggested Right Answers

As the number of strategic priorities expands, you must pay even more attention to the personal motivations of people. To do so:

1. *Align personal motivations with strategic priorities, not only in every key position but throughout the organization.*

2. *Beware of people who claim they can focus, equally well, on any and all strategic priorities; they're wrong.*

3. *Encourage a diversity of personal motivations that match the diversity of your organization's strategic priorities.*

4. *Don't expect everyone to share your own motivations.*

5. *Make sure you always know what motivates your people deep down.*

Applying Right Answers

The founder of a consulting firm at the age of 30 (I'll call her Hillary) had built it up over a 10-year period to include 22 professionals and a support staff of 5. The firm served a number of blue-chip clients with its innovative methodology for strategically designing growth-oriented structures. At age 40, Hillary dreamed of writing articles and books in which she could share her philosophy and experiences. "I'm really burnt out right now," she confessed. "I need a change of pace." However, since Hillary was the driving force behind the firm and its chief business developer, her absence could create a real hole. Despite her dream, she still wanted to gain a reputation and financial wealth that would attend a thriving consulting firm. Her three senior partners, who also owned shares in the company, convinced Hillary to remain focused on the singular task of building the company. Against her own innermost wishes, Hillary decided to remain involved in the business.

Unfortunately, as time went on, it became apparent that Hillary's motivation to build the company had deteriorated. For two years, the firm languished with mediocre results and an unclear plan about how to proceed in the future. While Hillary claimed she was doing the best she could, her partners began to believe that continuing to require Hillary to be the chief strategist and builder was not going to pay off. It was not, it seemed, in their own self-interest to force Hillary to do something she did not feel powerfully motivated to do.

At this point, Hillary and her partners developed a plan that would allow her to spend 75 percent of her time researching and writing and only 25 percent of her time in business development. One of the senior partners took over as chief executive officer, and Hillary became the chairman of the board. It didn't take long for the firm to resume much of its early excitement and vision for the future as the new CEO led it through its next stage of development. Hillary felt much more satisfied with her new role as she prepared to publish a book that could bring in a great deal of new business. By following her innermost motivation, she enjoyed the best of both worlds, launching a writing career while still helping her company prosper.

27

What Values Do People Hold Widely and Feel Deeply?

—————— ?❧ ——————

A few years ago, I sat in Professor Alan Wilkins's office at Brigham Young University, discussing his then forthcoming book *Developing Corporate Character*, in which the well-known corporate culture expert introduces the phrase "widely held and deeply felt values." During our chat, he pulled from his files a nicely printed sheet of paper containing a list of values. At the top of the page, I recognized the logo of a major corporation. As I read the list of values, I listened as Alan described how every person in this organization of over 200,000 employees had a copy of this list in his or her office, either tacked to the wall or tucked into their wallets. He said the values outlined on the sheet of paper really were widely held in this corporation. Everybody knew them and could recite them, but he expressed his belief that the values weren't deeply felt. He then described how you need both to have a great corporate culture. Since then, I have often reflected on the many value statements and mission statements I've seen throughout corporate America, and wondered whether the specified values were really deeply felt.

Kellogg's goal to attain 50 percent of the cereal market by 1992 ran into difficulties at the end of the last decade as Kellogg's cereals failed to keep pace with competitors' offerings, particularly in the oat bran area. Market share waned, expansion plans fell by the wayside, and the company lost millions in anticipated revenue. Such situations usually expose which values an organization holds widely and feels deeply. And that was just the case at Kellogg.

In response to the company's difficulties, the president and chief operating officer, Horst Schoeder, began taking the company and its people to task. In what many described as a demanding and abrasive manner, Schoeder called for the development of a new product every quarter, a demand that put enormous pressure on employees. As Schoeder pushed production teams to the breaking point, he made it clear that he wasn't interested in hearing any excuses or discussions of alternatives. This same authoritarian style came to bear as Schoeder interacted with the company's vice presidents, to whom he was seldom willing to listen and whom he regularly cut off in meetings of the senior team. Schoeder was also quick to confront people and issues, hanging a person out to dry if he or she wasn't up to his own high expectations. When things went well, he was also quick to take the credit, which didn't set well with the company's other executives.

Schoeder's primary motivation seemed worthy: to get the company back on top again. However, the values that motivated his actions did not synchronize with the Kellogg Way. Even though Schoeder had worked at Kellogg for 15 years, he did things his own way when he became president and heir apparent to the chairmanship. Ironically, it was Schoeder's comprehensive grasp of the business worldwide that had so impressed members of the Board of Directors in recent years. The Board believed Schoeder could really take the company to new heights. But now, after nine months as president, Schoeder was overriding the widely held and deeply felt Kellogg values of teamwork, consensus decision making, collegiality, and conformity. Did Schoeder's new value system offer a glimpse of the new heights Kellogg would eventually attain, or did it represent a dangerous aberration?

❧ The Key Question

Do you recognize, understand, and appreciate widely held and deeply felt values in your organization?

Kellogg's Answer

Horst Schoeder was fired on September 15, 1989. William La-Mothe, chairman and CEO, attributed the ouster to poor chemistry and philosophical differences. As it turned out, LaMothe's confidantes inside the company were keeping him abreast of Schoeder's "missteps" all along, a fact that in itself underscores the strong values that run through the 100-year-old cereal manufacturer. Even a president with the confidence of the Board of Directors and the charge to take the company to new heights can run into serious difficulty if he or she ignores the widely held and deeply felt values of the organization. Perhaps if Schoeder had been granted more time he could have reshaped Kellogg's corporate values, but while he was doing so, many of the company's best people may have left. In fact, William LaMothe admits that his concern over low morale and loyal people jumping ship or threatening to do so prompted Schoeder's firing.

Obviously, Schoeder had much to offer Kellogg, so how could he have avoided his termination? He had been extremely successful running the company's European, then the North American operations. Had he overreacted to the company's market share slump of 3 points? Did he try to move too fast? Did he fall victim to office politics and internal power plays? What would he do differently if he had the chance? Unfortunately, for Schoeder, these questions have become moot. You don't want that to happen to you.

Suggested Right Answers

To harness the most powerful motivating and culture-building force in any organization—widely held and deeply felt values— you can begin by doing the following:

1. *Identify the stories that people most often tell about the organization's recent and not-so-recent past.*

2. *Pinpoint the type of results that seem to receive the most praise: new products, new market entries, cost reductions, process innovations, steady performance, consistent practices, people development, satisfied customers, beaten competitors, etc.*

3. *Draw some conclusions about why people have been fired over the past few years.*

4. *Determine why people have been promoted over the past few years.*

5. *Combine your above lists to see what light they shed on widely held and deeply felt values.*

6. *Use your understanding of widely held and deeply felt values to determine whether to modify, change, or accelerate your own activities.*

Applying Right Answers

As the electric utility industry has changed in recent years, with more competition coming into the marketplace, one utility company struggled desperately to identify its strategic mission and the kind of management approach that could accomplish its goals. A newly appointed CEO wanted to get beyond the superficial mission statement that had guided the company in recent years and build a stronger internal culture for the years ahead. He gave the assignment to his director of Strategic Planning (I'll call him

Tom). Although Tom had a strong background in strategic and financial planning, he was somewhat of a novice when it came to looking at corporate values and culture. Still, he seemed to know intuitively what was really happening in the organization.

At the outset, Tom formed an internal task force to assess the company's current values. "I want you to dig beneath the surface to find out what's really motivating people in this organization," he told the group during their first meeting. "What do we care about? What do we worry about? What do we focus on day in and day out? What drives us?"

For his own part, Tom retained the services of a top consultant and attended a culture-building workshop that the consultant had designed for executives. Armed with a great deal of new insight and understanding, Tom helped his task force zero in on the true values that motivated behavior within the organization by examining oft-told war stories, patterns in hiring and firing, and the words with which people most commonly referred to the company and their own tasks.

After several months of interviewing, analysis, and assessment, Tom and his task force identified the single most important value that the firm had perpetuated: defensiveness and reactiveness. Because the public utility had come under great public scrutiny and criticism for rates, poor management, and pollution, the company had developed a siege mentality that affected everything it did. This mindset colored how people reported problems and financial performance, how they planned marketing programs, how they talked to customers, and how installation and repair crews organized and accomplished their work.

In the months afterwards, Tom analyzed the relationship between this value and the strategic position of the company, hoping finally to create a plan for moving into the next decade. Most importantly, he defined how the existing culture would have to shift the widely held and deeply felt value of defensiveness to one of actively meeting customer needs.

The CEO embraced Tom's plan, and for the first time in many years, the company began to make real progress as it went on the offensive. "If we act properly, anticipating customer needs and problems before they force us into a defensive stance, we can become more competitive," he announced early on. It took time, but as recruitment, promotion, and termination policies gained confidence with that mission, a truly remarkable change occurred. Customer complaints fell to an all-time low, morale rose considerably, and revenues and profits reflected a resurgence of what had once been a morbid organization. "It's funny," Tom recently commented, "but now people jokingly refer to our old culture as 'the tortoise.' We had a thick shell, and we were slow. Now we're the hare."

28

Do You Resist or Relish Change?

⊱

*H*ave you ever gone out to dinner with another couple and watched the following scene, or some variation thereof, unfold? The husband (it's just as often the wife) invariably coaxes his spouse to try something new, but the wife always sets her mind on her favorite dish. The husband, who relishes adventure and change, can't understand why his wife resists new things so strongly. Having seen this kind of interaction take place so often, I've concluded that people just don't alter their ingrained differences regarding change. I've seen it a lot in the corporate world, too.

Exxon continues to garner some deserved bad press for the oil spills, poor business decisions, and unproductive personnel practices that have plagued it recently. At the center of the storm stands Lawrence Rawl, chairman and CEO, with his own rather ingrained approach to change. Rawl, who wields an unusual amount of executive power, imposes his personal agenda for change on everyone else in the mammoth company, continuing to pursue a strategy that was right for the 1980s but may not work today. During and after the 1986 oil slump, most oil companies pursued retrenchment policies as they cut back on major outlays, such as exploration and reserve acquisition, and tried to ride out the crisis.

In the post-Gulf War era, however, the oil industry no longer wallows in a slump but has, in fact, been doing quite well. Strangely, Rawl has been continuing to maintain exploration and research outlays at low levels, to the point that Exxon is tapping oil reserves faster than it is acquiring new ones. Oil industry analysts say that such a track, if pursued for any length of time, will spell doom for Exxon, since Rawl's cost-cutting and retrenchment strategies have eliminated research on the vital technologies needed to both sustain Exxon's competitiveness and support a new U.S. energy policy. Massive staff reductions have placed burdensome workloads on those who remain with Exxon, and salary reductions, on top of the extra work and poor personnel practices, have knocked company morale to a new low, as both executives and employees complain about Exxon's direction. For his part, Rawl refuses to acknowledge work force problems and argues that morale is fine. Some critics blame the disastrous *Valdez* and other Exxon oil spills on the company's retrenchment, cutbacks, and morale problems, arguing that Rawl and his executives have perpetuated a serious flaw in the Exxon system that makes accidents more likely.

❧ The Key Question

Do you match people's feelings about change with their roles in the organization?

Exxon's Answer

Apparently, Exxon has chosen a "stabilizer and conservator" to set its priorities for the 1990s. Unfortunately, in a wildly changing world and a rapidly evolving industry, Rawl's inner motivations regarding change may not match Exxon's needs. According to many oil industry analysts, his posture will almost surely push his company into stagnation and decline. Rawl has garnered so much personal power by eliminating much of the consensus decision making that existed prior to his rise to the top that he can impose his own ideas about change on the entire company. Not surprisingly, and by his own admission, Rawl doesn't see much advantage in changing anything about himself.

Rawl's heir apparent and president of Exxon, Lee Raymond, appears to be cut from the same cloth as Rawl. If he also approaches change with Rawl's stabilizing attitude, Exxon could be in serious trouble by the end of the 1990s. Left to their own agendas and insulated from other voices, stabilizers and conservators can suck life out of an organization in need of enterprising change.

Suggested Right Answers

*When dealing with feelings about change, consider
the following points:*

1. *Rate your own attitude toward change as more stabilizing or more revolutionizing. What about those around you?*

2. *Assess how your attitude affects your career, your organization's performance, and your outlook for the future.*

3. *Determine how the feelings about change of those above and below you in the organization affect your job.*

4. *Decide whether staffing reassignments, additions, or terminations are necessary to bring feelings about change into line with the needs of your organization.*

5. *Beware of resisting necessary change; but also be wary of change for change's sake.*

Applying Right Answers

A senior executive for a large hotel and food service conglomerate (I'll call him Warren) was responsible for overseeing seven different food service divisions. One of them was giving him fits. Although its market had been changing rapidly, its president had dug in his heels, saying, "We'll weather this storm if we just stay to our course." Warren had challenged this view on several occasions, but nothing he said seemed to get through to the division president.

After a year and a half, during which the troubled division fell deeper and deeper below its competitors, Warren decided to let the division president go. Quickly, he brought in a new president known throughout the company as a bit of a revolutionary. It took only a year for the new head to bring about major changes in the division and start it on a rise from the depths.

To Warren's amazement, however, after the first 12 months a new set of problems emerged. The new president had literally turned things upside down when he took over, and that had seemed more than appropriate to Warren. But now he was turning things upside down again. Warren became increasingly alarmed by reports from within the division that the new president was destroying the new track he himself had established. Although Warren allowed him to continue over the next several months, he engaged him in a series of intense discussions about the need to stabilize an organization after massive changes have been injected into it. Ironically, these talks had no more effect than the ones with his predecessor.

Twenty-one months later, Warren removed the new division president, transferring him to another division within the group that needed change. Then, he set about the task of stabilizing the division that had gone through too many presidents in too short a time. Now Warren was looking for an individual with ideas about change somewhere between stabilizing and revolutionizing. He admitted that few other problems had so challenged him over the years. Too much change, not enough change, people who always resist change, people who can't live without change.

"I've learned to stress executive team flexibility more than anything else. Even the middle of the road can become a rut. People with different feelings about change need to learn to work together, allowing different change orientations to take center stage as needed."

29

Who's Motivated and Who's Not?

—————— ❧ ——————

*M*y wife, Pam, loves Egyptian history and has spent so much time studying and even visiting Egypt that she has become something of an amateur Egyptologist. Recently, she taught a three-week Egyptian history class for sixth-graders at our local elementary school, presenting artifacts and information that really brought Egypt to life for her students. The children participated enthusiastically, dressing up in Egyptian garb, creating props and displays about the subject, and even selecting one child to simulate a mummy in a home-made sarcophagus. On the last day of the course, the students donned costumes for an Egyptian party, during which they played the members of a Pharaoh's court. Delighted to see such tremendous motivation among the kids, their teachers complimented Pam extravagantly. I felt proud of her, too, and as I watched the enthusiasm of my daughter, who was a member of the class, I couldn't help but marvel at how much people can accomplish when they feel highly motivated.

Hibernia Corporation knows the value of motivation. A bank-holding company that dominates its markets in Louisiana and has outperformed many banks in the United States throughout a time when the financial services industry took a beating and many banks went belly-up, Hibernia provides an important lesson in the power of motivation as it averages 18 percent return on equity, 4 percent above the rest of the industry. The late 1980s and early 1990s have been hard on banks and while Hibernia has taken some lumps recently, its strength will certainly outlast less motivated bankers.

In 1973, Martin Miler took over as then-languishing Hibernia's CEO. The bank had fallen behind its two major competitors and sorely needed shoring up. For the next decade, Miler worked relentlessly to bring in the kind of people he could motivate to make the bank excellent. He shunned candidates who desired "banker's hours" or who couldn't roll up their sleeves and get their hands dirty. Miler himself often says, "We traded parade soldiers for foot soldiers." Aiming to make Hibernia unlike other banks, Miler seldom hired people from other banks where they might have learned bad habits. At Hibernia, people would not just sit back waiting for business to walk in the door but would go out after it aggressively. Over time, through attrition and careful hiring, Miler built a work force consisting of bankers who wanted to do more than their competitors. His conscious attempt to forge an aggressive sales-oriented work force where people got plenty of responsibility, along with strong cash incentives and stock options, pulled Hibernia out of its slump and set it a notch above most other banks in the country.

ᴥ The Key Question

How do you identify and evaluate the motivation levels of people in your organization?

Hibernia's Answer

Martin Miler and his executives make no bones about their wanting to be the best bank in the industry. In order to accomplish that objective, they must recruit people who want the same thing.

Wisely, however, Miler doesn't attempt to force his philosophy or his discipline on anyone else in the organization. He simply gives people the choice: If you want to work in an aggressive, results-oriented banking environment, welcome aboard; if not, you won't be happy here, you won't succeed here, and you'll be better off somewhere else. In the 17 years since Miler took over Hibernia, he has assembled a cadre of people deeply motivated to keep Hibernia Corporation on top. Earnings have climbed for 60 consecutive quarters. The company diversifies its risk, refusing to concentrate more than 5 or 10 percent of its loan capacity in any one industry. In order to keep the bank from becoming overly dependent on the volatile Louisiana economy, Hibernia makes 40 percent of its loans outside Louisiana. Officers base lending decisions on cash flows rather than on assets, making the company's loan portfolio one of the best performing in the industry. When it comes to acquisitions, of which Hibernia has completed many in recent years, it gravitates toward FDIC-assisted acquisitions, where bad loans have already been eliminated. When Hibernia makes an acquisition, it puts the new people through a rigorous program so they can decide whether they can muster the motivation that characterizes the Hibernia squad. By now, Hibernia executives have become pretty good at identifying who fits and who doesn't fit the company's high standards of motivation.

Suggested Right Answers

To discover levels of motivation, consider the signs of motivated people:

1. *They verbally express their motivation to others.*

2. *They outwardly act as if they are motivated.*

3. *They remain energized long after nonmotivated people have grown weary.*

4. *They do whatever it takes to get the job done.*

5. *They love their jobs.*

6. *They find creative ways to solve problems.*

7. *They get results.*

Applying Right Answers

A senior associate with an executive outplacement firm head-quartered in New York City (I'll call her Fran) was growing more and more frustrated with her firm's unwillingness to take a strong position with its clients, executives who ended up getting fired or pushed off coveted succession paths and wound up in her office recounting their sad stories.

Time and again she told her associates, "We don't look at moti-vation, or the lack of it, as the real reason why an otherwise talented individual fails." But her associates just shook their heads and said, "That's not *our* problem."

Fran, however, could not shake the belief that her job would be a lot easier if she got involved in efforts to address executives' levels of motivation earlier in their careers. Thinking about her own firm's reluctance to pioneer such an effort, Fran recognized that her own motivation had fallen out of alignment with the organization. Before long, she decided to start her own outplace-ment center.

At the outset, she refused to handle clients who just wanted her to deal with their terminated executives and managers, insisting instead that she help her clients identify motivation levels earlier in the process, before executives and managers lost their jobs. After retaining legal counsel specializing in employment practices to help make sure her programs conformed to the law, she began helping her clients focus on personal effectiveness and the mo-tivation that lay behind it. She felt certain that everyone would benefit from hiring, promotion, and firing decisions based on such a crucial underlying factor. As part of her firm's services, Fran began offering a workshop called "Building Motivated Executive Teams," that became an annual event for most of her clients. Finally, having aligned her own motivation, she could help her clients more than she ever had before. She recently told an associate, "I work harder for my own company than I ever did for the old firm. And you know What? I *love* every minute of it!"

30

Does Your Motivation Get Results?

— ❧ —

*I*t always amazes me to see people who, in the face of great adversity, rise above and conquer their circumstances. Some of the most poignant examples of such motivation come from people who have suffered severe injuries in automobile accidents. One of these is a 30-year-old man who was paralyzed from the waist down after a serious crash. Although doctors said he would never walk again, this individual simply would not give up, forcing himself through intense therapy and holding on to hope much longer than those around him. His motivation to overcome his circumstances enabled him, 10 years later, to walk normally. Recently, he participated in and finished a 10K marathon.

Phillips-Van Heusen tapped motivation to conquer financial woes brought about by intense competition in its industry. The manufacturer of shirts, sweaters, and shoes, which it sells through department and specialty stores around the world, also operates its own retail outlets under the name of "Profiles." A few years ago, the company was staggering under the weight of problems in the retail field, as well as a huge debt acquired when fending off a hostile takeover bid.

At that point, Lawrence S. Phillips, chairman and descendant of both the company's founders, instituted a new incentive plan for his 11-man executive team. Phillips knew exactly what kinds of results he wanted: earnings per share growth of 35% between 1988 and 1992, a rise from $1.05 to $3.48. In order to accomplish this goal, Phillips knew that his executives would have to pull together as never before, with each division helping every other division to make sure that the whole company could move forward.

By stating his expected results in such a specific fashion, Phillips hoped not only to focus management's concentration but also to smooth out the cyclical nature of earnings in his business. If Phillips-Van Heusen got those results, the stock price would rise from $8.00 to about $28.00 per share by 1992. If the company's 11 senior executives collectively achieved the earnings-per-share target within four years, each of them would receive a $1 million bonus. Would such an incentive provide sufficient motivation for the senior executive team to achieve the expected results?

❧ The Key Question

How do you get people in your organization sufficiently motivated to achieve desired results?

Phillips-Van Heusen's Answer

Two years into the plan, Phillips-Van Heusen proved to be doing very well. With earnings per share above $1.60, and the price of stock having gone as high as $25.00 per share, the senior team within Phillips-Van Heusen has made clear progress toward its goal. Stories of cooperation and teamwork now abound within the company. The 11 senior executives themselves have foregone all annual bonuses in an effort to attain the overriding earnings-per-share objective.

In one example of cooperative effort, the shirt and sweater divisions teamed up to produce appealing color-coordinated combinations that greatly boosted sales. In another, every manufacturing division has contributed to the design and positioning of the new Profiles outlets. Such cooperation, joint effort, and collective thinking epitomize the senior team at Phillips-Van Heusen, with each one striving not to let the others down. They view the pressure to reach their goal as quite positive, citing the fact that profits recently jumped 38 percent over the previous year. At a time when other suppliers to the retailing industry were suffering from an industry-wide malaise, Phillips-Van Heusen's performance really stands out. The 1991 recession has hurt company sales, but the executive team remains highly motivated.

Suggested Right Answers

When you're working to match motivation to results, consider these points:

1. *Make sure both existing motivations and desired results are clearly understood in your organization.*

2. *Recognize that motivation levels can be influenced as you attempt to bring motivations and results into alignment.*

3. *Don't hesitate to design creative incentive systems that will help boost the motivation of all people within your organization to achieve desired results.*

4. *Never expect low-level motivations to produce high-level results.*

5. *Don't stop until you've succeeded in increasing the level of motivation in yourself and others in your organization.*

6. *Make sure that your organization's increased motivation relates directly to its desired results.*

Applying Right Answers

Human resource people spend a lot of time thinking about motivation in organizations. A vice president of Human Resources for a medium-sized chemical plastics firm (I'll call him Byron) proposed to the chairman and CEO of the company that he develop a state-of-the-art compensation and incentive system geared to individual motivations within a group of 12 key executives. Byron believed deeply in the power of tailoring compensation and incentive systems to the needs of individuals, and he relished the thought of building a truly innovative one for his company. To his delight, the 73-year-old chairman and CEO, who had founded the company some 40 years earlier, gave Byron the green light to go ahead and do whatever he felt necessary to create a system that would better motivate his senior executives.

During the following months, Byron worked hard to gather solid data on the individual preferences and desires among the executive team and how those might change over the next few years. As he began to construct a menu of compensation and incentive possibilities from which individuals could choose for themselves, Byron could see that the majority of the executives desired both growth for the company and gradual ownership through stock options or some other program. While they expressed different motivations, they agreed that they should reinvest profits in the company near term in order to gain the desired growth and development over the next decade.

Assembling all the data, Byron designed a set of options for the executives, all basically oriented toward growth, coupled with ownership over a 20-year span. When a buoyant Byron presented the plan to the chairman, he couldn't believe his ears as the man shared with Byron his own desire to cash himself out of the company by selling out to a larger firm. The chairman confessed that he had not discussed this idea with his executives because he had only recently begun thinking seriously about his own retirement. With no heirs interested in participating in the business long-term, he had concluded that he could best meet his own and his family's needs by selling the company. Of course, that meant getting the best possible price in the short-term, which in turn meant enhancing the immediate earnings and changing the capital structure of the company, goals that ran completely counter to the executive team's desire for long-term growth.

After so many months of work, Byron realized that he had failed to account for the most important motivation in the company, that of the founder and majority shareholder. Now a significant mismatch existed between those motivations and his brilliant new plan. Byron kicked himself for not paying more attention to the chairman's needs, but perhaps, he thought, he could still save the day. Over the next several months, he worked with the executive team to engineer a management buy-out that met both the chairman's needs and the desires of his subordinates. It took a full two years to accomplish, but it turned out well in the end because Byron unfailingly attended to everyone's motivations and desires for results.

Part VII

TRUST

❧

31

Do You Maintain Clear Strategic Vision?

৵

*D*uring a recent family vacation, my family and I were trying to find an amusement park our children wanted to visit. After driving for much longer than we had anticipated, the kids began complaining that I didn't know where I was going. I assured them that I had things under control. "Trust me," I said. That quieted everyone down for several minutes, but soon the complaints began again. "Trust me," I insisted. "I know where I'm going!" Fifteen minutes later, still not having found the park, I began to wonder whether I really did know where I was going. With my children growing more and more impatient and my wife urging me to stop and ask for directions, I pulled into a gas station. To my chagrin, I had been going in the wrong direction and had to backtrack to the amusement park, which we finally reached 40 minutes later. My wife and children gave me a hard time about that incident for the rest of our vacation. "Trust me!" one would shout, and they'd all break into hysterics. Later, I could laugh about it myself, yet I reflected seriously on how easily you can lose the trust of people in an organization when you fail to maintain clear vision.

Norwest Corporation illustrates the point. Not long ago, Norwest was a troubled financial services institution with overextended foreign loans and an unprofitable morgage-lending business.

When the future for Norwest looked the bleakest, Lloyd Johnson came aboard from Security Pacific National Bank. As the new CEO, he predicted that the company would rebound and reach new heights of profitability and return on equity. To fulfill that prophecy, Johnson created an unwavering strategic vision for the company, which included a retrenching, back-to-banking-basics policy and an emphasis on retail banking in the more than 250 communities that it served across the Midwest.

While Johnson's strategic vision may have lacked glamor, it was nevertheless steady and sure. Under its mandate, the company sold off its mortgage-banking business, stopped competing for corporate loans, and reduced its foreign-lending vulnerability. At the same time, Norwest's consumer finance and retail-banking business became centerpieces of the restructured organization. Johnson bestowed more central control to the company's credit policy, a move that people within the organization readily accepted as their confidence in Johnson's clear strategic vision grew stronger and stronger. Johnson remained steadfast in his devotion to his risk aversion and go-slow strategy, believing that such a game plan would solidly position Norwest as the premier retailing bank in the region. All along the way, people understood what he was trying to do and, as a result, felt comfortable placing their trust in both the man and his vision.

ᴇ▲ The Key Question

How do you make sure your strategic vision is clear enough to engender trust in everyone in the organization?

Norwest's Answer

What did all of this clarity of strategic vision produce at Norwest? In less than five years, Norwest's return on equity rose to more than 19 percent. Earnings per share rose more than 31 percent, and profits grew to $237 million, a 12 percent increase in a single year. All this makes the Norwest turnaround one of the most low-key and unheralded turnarounds in recent business experience. The company expects to maintain double-digit growth rates in the years ahead, without a lot of acquistions, by pursuing the strategic vision that Lloyd Johnson launched in 1986.

Suggested Right Answers

When clarifying strategic vision, consider these rules of thumb:

1. *Don't let your organization's strategic vision waiver. Every time it does, the trust and confidence of your organization's people also waivers.*

2. *Make sure your organization is prepared for changes in strategic vision when they come. The trust level of people will drop, unless they clearly and precisely understand, recognize, and accept the reasons for the change.*

3. *Make your organization's strategic vision visible and relevant to what people are doing every day; otherwise it won't build trust.*

4. *Take the necessary steps to ensure that the people who work closely with you are not hesitant in any way about discussing the expected results of your organization's strategic vision, or the trust level among people will wane.*

5. *The most important thing you can do is to maintain the clarity and constancy of your organization's strategic vision in order to maximize trust.*

Applying Right Answers

We all know cases of people struggling in organizations that lack clear strategic vision. One such case was an accounting manager in a Fortune 500 company (I'll call him Eric). For a number of years, his firm had teetered on the brink of bankruptcy, until it was finally gobbled up by an even larger company. The new parent quickly liquidated all the operations it could not salvage.

Eric described his day-to-day experiences during the years prior to the acquisition, when the company had pretty much hit bottom: "The days passed so slowly, I felt like my life and my career had come to a complete standstill. No one seemed to know what was going on, but rumors were flying everywhere. One day, the board was going to fire the CEO, the next day the CEO was doing a leveraged buyout. None of it was true, but we ate it all up like starving orphans. I remember going to the cafeteria at lunch and listening to people talk about dusting off their resumés and looking for new jobs. Most people were afraid of being laid off without warning, and senior managers worried openly about career stagnation. We all had a sinking feeling that the terrible reputation of the company would stay with us for the rest of our lives.

"As I thought about what was happening and talked it all over with co-workers, I realized that the trust level in the place had slipped below zero. While you'd gobble up any new rumor, no matter how outrageous, in your heart you wouldn't believe anything you heard. The CEO would call corporate staff meetings in the cafeteria to try to allay our concerns about the company's future, but people would actually poke each other in the ribs and say things like, 'Sure, and pigs can fly.' For days afterwards, everyone would mumble about the CEO's lies and stupidity. It became a disease, infecting almost every relationship you had with people above and below you. Before the takeover, I was losing sleep, and my wife made me see a doctor. It turned out I had an incipient ulcer. I couldn't believe it. I hadn't been sick in years, and now my job was literally killing me. That's when I quit."

Eric's account may sound extreme, but far too many organizations cause the same kinds of mental and physical anguish, quite often because they have become strategically bankrupt and devoid of trust. It's usually wise to exit the scene before they become financially bankrupt as well.

32

Are You Trustworthy?

❧

*T*rust. We all value it, though few of us can explain exactly how you win it or why you lose it. Most of us do know, however, that a tiny slip, an unguarded comment, a rash remark, a thoughtless gesture, or some other seemingly insignificant occurrence can greatly affect people's trust. I remember one incident in which a director in a large organization was sitting in his boss's office, a vice president of the organization, when the latter took a call from another vice president. As this director eavesdropped on his boss's conversation, he marveled at how pleasant and cooperative his boss seemed. That was the sort of open, honest composure he hoped to develop in himself. To his astonishment, the instant his boss hung up the phone, he rattled off a string of expletives, calling the other vice president several unrepeatable names. Having vented his anger, he smiled at the director and said, "Let's get back to work." That few seconds unalterably affected the director's view of his boss's trustworthiness. From that day on, he felt he could never fully trust what his boss said to his face. "How do I know," he wondered, "that he doesn't call *me* names behind my back."

The people who work for Joseph A. Cannon, chairman and CEO of Geneva Steel Corporation, have no such problem. After Cannon and his associates bought the Geneva steel mill from USX in

1987, they quickly turned it into one of the most profitable companies in the steel industry. A lot of the success stems from the trust that Joe Cannon has imbued into his senior executive team and all of the more than 2700 workers at Geneva Steel. When Joe makes a promise, he sticks to it. Consequently, his people have come to believe what he says. Joe seems to know instinctively that no other factor does more to strengthen a corporate culture. From the beginning, he told workers that he had not taken over the company to make a financial killing, buying the mill at a low price and then selling it for top dollar once he made it profitable. Rather, he wanted to build something solid and lasting. He delivered on that promise by investing some $200 million to modernize the steel mill, making it one of the most low-cost steel-manufacturing outfits in the world. He also came through on a promise that workers would get a chance to share in the profits and ownership of the company. When the company went public in 1990, those opportunities became a reality. As the company encounters inevitable crises, Joe Cannon immediately assembles his people and tells them exactly what is happening. As a result, employees at Geneva Steel have come to trust Joe Cannon.

❧ The Key Question

How do you attain trustworthiness?

Joe Cannon's Answer

For Joe Cannon, the answer is simple. He speaks his mind and shuns hidden agendas, and by doing so he encourages similar honesty and openness at all levels of the organization. Many in his organization describe him as a man without guile.

Recently, the company experienced a community crisis as local residents complained about the negative environmental impact of the plant. As the crisis escalated in the media, Joe handled it all straightforwardly, promising that Geneva Steel would do its part to clean up the air and keep the steel mill within safe limits. Joe Cannon's experience as a former director in the Environmental Protection Agency in Washington, D.C., certainly aided him as he tried to communicate exactly what Geneva would do to shoulder its environmental responsibility. After he proposed spending $20 million on clean air programs, he made good on his promise. What might have turned into a calamity for Geneva dissipated slowly and smoothly as Joe Cannon brought his trustworthiness to bear on the situation. While Geneva continues to receive criticism from clean air fanatics, no critic has been able to impugn Joe Cannon's integrity or trustworthiness.

Suggested Right Answers

If you want to increase the trust in your organization, increase your trustworthiness first:

1. *Be honest and open with everyone.*

2. *Don't make promises you can't keep.*

3. *Keep all of the promises you make.*

4. *If circumstances beyond your control make it impossible for you to keep a promise, then make sure everyone understands the circumstances and what you will do now.*

5. *Don't follow hidden agendas; in fact, don't even entertain thoughts about such agendas.*

6. *When you can't share certain information with your people, tell them why you can't.*

7. *Hire and promote trustworthy people.*

8. *Counsel or fire people who exhibit untrustworthy behavior.*

Applying Right Answers

The director of research for a medium-sized consumer products company (I'll call him David) felt he could not fully trust his boss, the vice president of R&D, who on too many occasions had twisted information to further his own advantage. This tendency bothered David because he himself felt deeply committed to the company and would probably have to confront his boss about this issue sooner or later.

The opportunity to do so came earlier than David expected, at an annual planning meeting attended by both his boss and the president of the company. This management retreat, held at a resort just south of San Diego, was designed to solidify plans and forecasts for the next three years. David was aghast when his boss presented a new product development schedule that David knew could not possibly be accomplished. Given his boss's tendency under pressure to say what he thought others wanted to hear, David felt certain that his boss was simply buying time with his bogus projections. David decided to confront the issue because failure to achieve the dishonest schedule would reflect badly on the entire R&D function—David included. Worse, it would hurt the company's credibility in the marketplace.

David chose not to say anything during the first day, hoping someone else might point out the flaw in the projections. When no one did, David considered his options. Should he blow the whistle on his own boss, he could be writing his own pink slip. Ultimately, however, he decided to approach the president of the company that very evening. A little after ten o'clock, he and the president left the hotel for a walk along the beach, during which David confessed how he felt about his boss, not just in this instance but in three or four others over the past year, all of which underscored the man's untrustworthiness. Initially, the president reacted with skepticism, grilling David for details on his accusations. Though David felt very uncomfortable, he stuck to his guns, because he believed doing so was in the best interests of the company. After an hour-long discussion, the president dismissed David, asking him to be patient while he decided how to respond to the situation.

Since the president had been CEO of the organization only for a year, he did not know all of the history of the company and its people. Perhaps David had his own axe to grind with the R&D VP. Therefore, he undertook his own probing to test David's accusations. Cautiously and discreetly, he talked with other VP's during the second day of the meeting, and by the end of the retreat, he told David he would tackle the issue as soon as the management group returned to their corporate offices.

News of the confrontation spread quickly, with the startling rumor that the VP had actually broken down in tears over his feelings of fear and inadequacy. Everyone in R&D waited to see what would happen. Had the president fired their boss? As it turned out, he hadn't, but he had caused a dramatic change in the VP's behavior. The VP called his troops together, told them he wanted to emphasize openness and honesty in the group, and said the first step in this direction would be to fully revise any unrealistic projections to bring them in line with reality. To David, it was a welcome change, and he quickly set aside his misgivings and gave his boss his full support. Old habits don't die easily though and the VP of R&D struggled over the next year to fulfill his promise of total trustworthiness. Still, he made such substantial progress he not only kept his job but he won the respect of his whole department. As David expressed it, "Trust is contagious. We get it from each other." I'm sure the president of his company would agree.

33

Do You Keep the Borders to Change Open?

≈

An acquaintance of mine recently quit his job without notice. A division vice president for a major company, he seemed to have been on a fast-track to the top. When I asked him why, he said, "I was on a treadmill going nowhere." He went on to say that the company could not accept any of the ideas or innovations he proposed for his division. As a result, he felt frustrated and unhappy, despairing over the fact that he could do nothing to keep the commitment to his job.

In my experience, when an organization closes the borders to change, not only can commitment vanish, but trust as well. My friend quit because he thought his supervisors didn't trust him. He paid them back with his own form of distrust when he quit. Too often executives think that trust is only a function of constancy and consistency, while in reality, as my friend's experience shows, it can be a function of change.

At Royal Dutch Shell, a company that exemplifies the learning organization, a lot of trust regarding the future of the company has sprung up because management keeps the borders to change open. Shell's willingness to embrace change has been heralded by business media articles, with much praise heaped on its planning and learning ability. According to Arie P. DeGeus, head of

Planning for Shell, Shell does not create plans, it changes minds. He points out that the company encourages people to create scenarios, playing "what if" games that relate to the future. With everyone in the organization building scenarios for change, the trust level has shot skyward. People know they are not going to be taken by surprise when change does occur.

Change has become a vital part of life at Shell and runs throughout the fabric of the organization. For example, in 1984, when oil prices ran near $28 per barrel, Shell asked all of its executives worldwide to envision a future in which prices fell to $15 per barrel. Then each officer responded to certain tough questions. "What do you think your government will do?" "What do you think your competition will do?" "What, if anything, will you do?" While no one expected this scenario to actually happen, Royal Dutch Shell executives nevertheless played along with the game throughout 1985. When, in 1986, oil prices unexpectedly did fall, first to $17, then to $10, the company took it in stride. The border to change had remained open, and according to Shell chairman, L.C. Van Wachem, "There was no panic."

❧ The Key Question

How do you keep the borders to change open and feelings of trust solid?

Shell's Answer

Surprisingly, Royal Dutch Shell is run by a committee. And in this case, the committee has designed a race horse, not a camel. At a time when other oil companies were cutting back, retrenching and still fearing the threat of the oil price drops of 1986, Royal Dutch Shell replenished its oil reserves through exploration and acquisition faster than it could possibly use those reserves, at a rate well over 125 percent. After the Iraqi invasion of Kuwait,

Shell, fully prepared for such contingencies in the Middle East, had already been working hard to make itself independent, with plentiful reserves and an $8 billion cash surplus. Clearly, the committee at the top, the Executive Committee, wrote some pretty accurate scenarios that kept the borders to change wide open. Because thinking about the future has become such an integral part of everyday life at Shell, it has created an amazing level of trust among employees and managers throughout the organization. This has, in turn, established great self-reliance among employees and managers as they freely traverse the borders of change and discover the future.

Suggested Right Answers

As you evaluate your organization's attitude toward the borders to change, you should:

1. *Remember that you must establish predictability to* **gain** *trust.*

2. *Predict ways in which people will have to change in the future to* **increase** *trust.*

3. *Make change a constant part of your organization and your people's attitudes to* **maintain** *trust.*

4. *Remember that effective change* **breeds** *trust, trust breeds self-reliance, and self-reliance breeds accountability for results.*

Applying Right Answers

Not long ago, a major crisis struck a medium-sized metal fabricating company. It came from two directions at once: The price of its main supply, rolled steel, shot up, and its largest customer got shot down and had to seek Chapter 11 bankruptcy protection. As a result, the president of the fabricating company was putting a lot of pressure on everyone to make adjustments, such as slashing costs and securing new customers. The company's national sales manager (I'll call him John) had only assumed his job 18 months earlier. John was scared because he couldn't predict exactly what the president would do in this crisis, and he started scrambling to find new customers to fill the void when its customer in Chapter 11 cut orders by two-thirds. Even if the customer worked its way out of Chapter 11, it would not resume its previous ordering level for at least another two to three years.

With the president demanding short-term results in the form of new customers, John grew increasingly desperate because he knew how long it took to cultivate new customers. If potential buyers sensed panic, they would take even longer to convince. Complicating matters even further, John believed the company should broaden its customer base so it would not be so vulnerable to one customer's problems.

Finally, John found a major potential customer, a heating and cooling equipment manufacturer, that could save the day. If John could win it over, it would strongly influence a whole group of customers that needed the same kind of product. Unfortunately, the metal fabrication these customers needed was one that John's company had been unable to perfect. Now it fell upon John to persuade the president of his company to renew the effort to perfect that process or risk losing the new customers.

Much to John's chagrin, the president blew up when he heard how John had been spending his time, accusing him of ignoring the crisis by irresponsibly trying to bring in business that required retooling the manufacturing process. John left the president's office bewildered. The market was changing, but John's boss wouldn't let the company change with it. As far as John was concerned, if the company stayed in its same old rut, unwilling to adapt to the needs of different kinds of customers, it would just go through an identical crisis again in the future. John's trust in the president of the company deteriorated, and it hit rock bottom when a key salesman who reported to John resigned. While a general feeling of hopelessness had fallen over the entire sales force, the president continued applying more and more pressure, with less and less effect. Eventually, the company had to cut back drastically on a number of fronts just to stay in business. John, unable to muster up much faith in the company's future, and unable to deal with the lack of trust that had infected his relationship with the president, himself resigned and went to work for a competitor. His former company is now attempting to avoid bankruptcy itself.

34

Do You Strive for Consistency and Reliability?

— ❧ —

*E*veryone knows certain people who exude consistency and reliability, the sort of people who instill immediate and deep trust. For me, one such person is Curtis Van Alfen, a professor of educational leadership, whose depth of peace, contentment, and sense of self-worth touches all around him. He maintains such a firm hold on himself that even in the midst of crisis he radiates strength and dependability. At his core he is consistent and reliable. It comes as no surprise, then, that his associates, friends, and students trust him implicitly. The best executives build trust the same way, while the worst ones never do get the hang of it.

Take Robert Campeau, the Canadian businessman who acquired Allied Stores for $3.6 billion and then Federated Department Stores for $6.5 billion, only to watch the two retailing giants plunge into bankruptcy less than two years later. What caused this chain of events: Bob Campeau's inconsistent and unreliable behavior. Campeau's salesmanship seemed to build trust quickly with bankers, investors, advisors, and clients—allowing him to convince key people at Citicorp, First Boston, Dean Witter, Equitable Life Assurance, and Prudential Insurance to jump on his bandwagon. Behind that convincing veneer, however, lay an unstable and untrustworthy soul. The sums paid for Allied Stores and Federated Department Stores were, in retrospect, unthinkable and would not likely happen today. Those were the 1980s, though, a decade characterized by greed and self-gain. In that environment, a long list of bankers, investment advisors, attorneys, and corporate executives joined with Bob Campeau in his excessively overleveraged adventure without taking time to discover Bob Campeau's underlying instability.

It wouldn't have taken much. With a track record of emotional breakdowns, volatile behavior, and excessively aggressive business practices, Bob Campeau sent out plenty of warning signals. Divorce, a mistress, children born out of wedlock, and other signs of personal unreliability should have caused second thoughts among competent executives and counselors thinking of doing business with Campeau. Nevertheless, Bob Campeau was able to raise extraordinary amounts of money to buy Allied and Federated, burdening them with a level of debt they could never possibly service, even during the best of times. Only when Allied Stores and Federated Department Stores entered Chapter 11 bankruptcy in January 1990 was Bob Campeau removed from a position of influence in the retailing operations of the two companies.

❧ The Key Question

Do you use consistency and reliability to engender trust?

Robert Campeau's Answer

Bob Campeau epitomized the excessive living and volatile deals of the 1980s. Unfortunately, he inflicted great pain on many innocent victims. Hundreds of thousands of vendors and suppliers have lost money, over 100,000 employees lost their jobs, and the ripple effects of Allied and Federated's bankruptcy on the industry and local economies will be felt years in the future by countless people and institutions. Every one of us can make mistakes and, hopefully, Bob Campeau can find some way to redeem and restore himself in the years ahead. However, none of us should expect to engender trust in others when our own track record of effectiveness remains unreliable and inconsistent.

Suggested Right Answers

The following tips will help you increase your own, as well as others', individual effectiveness with respect to consistency and reliability:

1. *Never place your trust in anyone who does not display consistent values, priorities, and goals that you deem appropriate and worthwhile.*

2. *Don't ever be afraid to challenge the consistency and reliability of those seeking your trust.*

3. *Don't let anyone tell you that abstract, ethical, and moral issues deserve no place in business endeavors.*

4. *Whenever you develop serious questions about the reliability of someone you trust, resolve your concerns immediately.*

5. *Look for the signs that indicate a lack of values, such as selfishness, greed, and abuse of power.*

6. *Remember that personal effectiveness based on consistency and reliability, even when that consistency includes constant change, builds trust, and that trust fuels greater effectiveness.*

Applying Right Answers

A division president for a large corporation (I'll call him Richard) had followed his boss up the corporate ladder through three promotions over a 10-year span. Richard and his boss worked so well together, Richard didn't mind tying his star to someone else's, especially someone with such a strong sense of where he was going and what he wanted to accomplish with the company. As the company grew through acquisitions and mergers, Richard's boss grew with it, pulling Richard along in his wake. Most people figured that before long, Richard's boss would end up running the entire corporation, and that suited Richard just fine. For the time being, however, he was content as a division president under his boss, the group vice president overseeing eight divisions.

That contentment began to dissolve, however, as Richard began seeing discomforting events in his boss's personal life. Richard knew his boss was going through an ugly divorce, but so were a lot of other people Richard knew, so he just chalked up the occasional smell of alcohol on his boss's breath early in the morning as just a temporary aberration. At one time, Richard and his wife, Kathy, had often seen his boss and his wife socially, but that had come to a halt with the divorce. Richard seldom saw his boss away from work. At the office, Richard's boss began to miss certain critical deadlines, and he more and more forgot to meet other commitments. This behavior was so uncharacteristic Richard simply attributed it to his boss's temporary personal difficulties, believing that it would soon pass.

As time went on, the performance of some of the divisions in his boss's group began to falter, and Richard found himself coming under increasing pressure to bolster his division's sagging performance. Richard did all he could to increase the performance of his own division, but he felt more and more ineffective without his boss's steady guidance. Imagine his shock when he returned from a two-week business trip to find that his boss had resigned with no warning whatsoever. In fact, nobody in the company even knew where his boss had gone. Although Richard had been in line to succeed his boss as group vice president, the job went to another division president who had distanced himself from Richard's boss much earlier.

Richard tried to fight off the bitterness he felt toward his boss for letting him down, but sadly he only came to grips with it a year later when he learned that his boss had performed the ultimate act of instability by taking his own life.

35

Does Trust Produce Results?

— ૨ૡ —

*I*n the movie *Hoosiers*, Gene Hackman starred as a basketball coach who had been banned from college athletics for striking one of his players but eventually landed a coaching job in a small Indiana town. The team wasn't much to brag about, especially since its star player refused to play. Hackman, drawing on his knowledge of the game and his deep devotion to it, inspired the players and convinced the star to come back. In the process, he put together a team that came out of nowhere to win the state title. Why did the star player, who had sworn off basketball, decide to play? Why did the other players on the team produce such unbelievable results? Because they trusted their coach, and he trusted them. When trust runs high, it really can produce amazing results.

Rod Canion built Compaq Computer Corporation on that sort of trust. Customers, dealers, employees, and Wall Street analysts trust what Canion says and what the Compaq organization promises. As a result, in seven years, the company reached $3 billion in sales. Compaq has not succeeded by building innovative new products, but by borrowing others' technology and making sensible improvements in production and marketing. While other companies field direct sales forces, Compaq has continued to work through dealerships, cementing a bond of trust with dealers by moving their products exclusively through the dealership system. Customers have benefitted from Compaq's strategy to deliver dependable machines at affordable prices.

Rod Canion pays as much attention to how people treat each other within the Compaq organization as he does to how they produce and sell computers. He meets each quarter with his headquarter employees, bringing them up to speed on company developments and answering questions, no matter how difficult. Management arrives at decisions by consensus in an environment where no one shies away from airing any problem or concern. Defensiveness and disruptive office politics seldom occur at Compaq because such great trust exists among management and employees throughout the organization.

❧ The Key Question

Can you relate the trust in your organization to results?

Compaq's Answer

During seven years of phenomenal growth, Compaq enjoyed the enviable position of being the only major U.S. computer firm that had not suffered a bad stumble. In the fourth quarter of 1989, however, earnings were looking so sluggish that Rod Canion worried that the news could send the stock tumbling. During the boom years, it had been easy for him to be open with Wall Street analysts, but could he maintain that openness in this earnings crisis?

Consistent with the company's trust-building policy, even before the troubled quarter ended, Canion came forth with the bad news so that no investors would be hurt by a sudden announcement, months from then, that might devalue their investments. While Compaq's stock did drop $8.50 per share, a 16 percent decline, no one could accuse the company of withholding vital information. As the quarter ended, it turned out that the earnings decline was not as bad as some analysts had imagined, with profits actually decreasing only 14 percent. As that news hit Wall Street, the stock jumped $3.00. Looking back, analysts describe Rod Canion's handling of the situation as honorable and trustworthy. His approach worked in Compaq's favor, stabilizing the stock after the November announcement and then allowing it to jump back up in February 1990. As Rod Canion demonstrated, trust works, not just in good times but in bad times as well.

Suggested Right Answers

Think about the following as you evaluate the relationship between trust and results in your own organization:

1. *Always respect the truth.*

2. *Work to shatter illusions and false hopes.*

3. *Recognize that trust aids successful performance and vice versa.*

4. *Never shade the truth in times of crisis.*

5. *Be patient.*

6. *Cherish trust because it can be destroyed in an instant.*

Applying Right Answers

The following account describes three attorneys (I'll call them Tom, Bob, and Sam) who had been lifelong friends and decided after several years of working in separate practices to join together in their own firm. Tom, Bob, and Sam each brought a particular legal expertise to the new endeavor, and to start it up, they obtained some debt financing that included putting up their own homes as collateral. Immediately, they hired an office manager and three junior associates. Their strategic goal was to instill a degree of unity to the management of the firm that seldom occurred in the field of law. That goal hinged, of course, on the strong bond of trust that already existed between them.

Early on, although the firm enjoyed a certain amount of success, Bob and Tom began to realize that Sam was falling short of the expectations each of them had laid out. However, the two felt reluctant to raise the issue with Sam because it might violate the trust that bound them together. As the months went on and expenses mounted, Sam's performance became more and more a sore point. He simply was not developing enough clients and billable hours to justify his position with the firm. Basically, Tom and Bob were carrying Sam.

When they finally did confront their partner, Sam became defensive, accusing Tom and Bob of trying to squeeze him out. Needless to say, the lifelong friendship began unraveling. In the weeks that followed, they talked it all over several times, but all the discussion did little but leave all three feeling betrayed. Eventually, Tom put it to Sam this way: "Trust only works when it's based on reality and results, and your unwillingness to face up to the reality of unacceptable results is destroying our friendship." To that, Sam retorted, "You've got to give me time. I can make it, but you have to be patient. Trust me." Tom responded, "I can't."

And so that's where the impasse stood, with the three partners unable to come to any reasonable resolution. In the end, after the three had no choice but to admit that their friendship was damaged beyond repair, Tom and Bob bought out Sam's share of the company and gave him a handsome severance package. Tom and Bob went on to build a successful firm which employees could trust to treat them fairly and compassionately, and the firm could trust the employees to perform and grow. Sam did reasonably well on his own, too, but he never did take on a partner.

Part VIII

TECHNOLOGY

36

Do You Apply Strategically Appropriate Technology?

——————— ❧ ———————

*O*ne Sunday morning I was looking forward to attending a Gospel doctrine class taught by a man with a great mind and a humble spirit. When I arrived, I was surprised to see a VCR television monitor and overhead projector in the front of the room and a stack of handouts generated by a home computer. Why all the gadgets, I wondered? Looking more closely at his handouts, I saw that they contained a lot of computer commands that distracted the eye from key information the instructor wanted us to study. I could tell that he was just learning how to operate his home computer and printer. By the end of the lesson, he had miscued the tape on the VCR, had not been able to get the monitor to work the first time, and had smeared the overhead transparencies, making them difficult to read. Oddly, his reliance on all that instructional technology had compromised his ability to deliver a great lesson. Still, I gained a valuable insight from the experience: Technology doesn't necessarily or automatically improve your ability to obtain desired objectives.

In the business world, Frito-Lay has always maintained a strategic edge in technology. A few years ago, Frito-Lay executives conceived of a hand-held computer system that would allow their more than 10,000 salespeople to feed in data from their various locations throughout the day. Immediately updating the control data base, the company could use the information to help it respond more effectively to customer buying trends and store-stocking needs. Ultimately, this technology promised to make the company's famed store-door delivery system even more effective and efficient.

The store-door system, which uses company vans to insure smooth product flow, has allowed Frito-Lay to maintain a strong advantage in the snack food business, and the hand-held computer innovation bolstered that advantage because it was strategically appropriate. That's a key phrase: *strategically appropriate*. Strategically appropriate technology gets the job done efficiently and cost effectively, while advancing the company's strategic advantage. In the case of Frito-Lay, the enhanced data goes to senior executives who track overall corporate, market, and industry trends and to department heads, division heads, and manufacturing supervisors who track all the movement of products in different markets, making Frito-Lay ever more responsive to customer needs.

ᔥ The Key Question

How do you determine the strategic appropriateness of new technologies?

Frito-Lay's Answer

At Frito-Lay, the application or development of technology always depends on its strategic value. Will a new technology contribute to the growth or well-being of the organization? Does it strike at the very heart of what makes Frito-Lay tick? The hand-held computer system certainly met those requirements, since it strengthened Frito-Lay's main competitive advantage. The company didn't jump at the technology for its own sake but because it embodied a state-of-the-art decision support system that could make it even more unbeatable, both nationally and worldwide, in snack food markets. Strategically appropriate technology at Frito-Lay strengthens the company's vital strategic position.

Suggested Right Answers

Before you make any major investments in new technology, weigh the following considerations:

1. *Determine whether any new technology, any modification or new application of recently developed technology will allow you to better satisfy existing or future customer needs.*

2. *Consider whether a particular technology will significantly increase your ability to capitalize on a longstanding company strength or develop a needed new company strength.*

3. *Evaluate whether a new technology will increase your ability to sustain or enhance competitive advantages.*

Applying Right Answers

Recently a group of management consultants switched from an IBM-based secretarial pool to Macintosh computers in every consultant's office. The group formed the entire management consulting arm of a "Big 8" accounting firm in a large metropolitan city, and one of their younger members (I'll call him Daniel) changed their work habits forever. Of course, some new technology was also involved. Daniel had only been with the firm for one year, but he felt certain that the Macintosh system, which he knew inside out, would increase the group's computer utilization by 50 percent. Not only would people who shied away from the more-difficult-to-use IBMs love the Macs, but those already accustomed to working on computers would use the Macs even more.

It took a year to accomplish the changeover and get everyone up to speed on the new machines, mostly Macintosh SEs or SE-30s, at the time. But once that switchover and training had occurred, four important things happened: Billable hours increased, the number of clients increased, and client satisfaction improved. Since the company obviously valued these variables highly, management determined the switchover a success, and Daniel was soon in great demand at other offices within the firm.

The Mac technology was appropriate, it turned out, because it enabled consultants to prepare materials, reports, analyses, and graphics more productively. The system circumvented the need for staff support, long waiting periods, and turnaround time. It allowed consultants to deal with more clients, it shortened engagement times, and it made consultants more responsive to clients. All these factors contributed directly to client satisfaction. The consultants also found themselves growing more and more creative in their presentations of data, analyses, and recommendations because the Mac facilitated effective graphics. To his credit, Daniel knew, even in his first year on the job, that if a technology could make the consultants more efficient and effective in meeting client demands, it would create a strong strategic advantage. "I don't put down IBM," David said recently. "They're appropriate for lots of situations. But here, the strategically appropriate technology is spelled M-A-C."

37

Does Your Culture Embrace New Technology?

_____ ੨♠ _____

*A*pplied wisely, technology can increase an organization's power. However, the internal culture must respond to appropriate technology in just the right way. A recent television commercial shows a woman vowing that she will never use a personal computer to do her work. Clearly, the machines intimidate her. As the commercial proceeds, she finally tries the new technology and enthusiastically incorporates it into her job. By the end of the commercial, she has become a vocal computer fan. I imagine that commercial is effective because it hits a nerve among many office workers who fear new technology.

Caterpillar, one of the excellent companies of the early 1980s, had to conquer that sort of fear when it desperately needed new technology. As the largest manufacturer of heavy tractor and farm machinery in the world, Caterpillar had developed a strong organizational culture, greatly admired for its attention to customer needs and its emphasis on service. Unfortunately, the Caterpillar culture did not eagerly embrace new technology on the manufacturing side, and the company eventually found itself weighted down with antiquated manufacturing and assembly systems in all its plants. Although efficient, the systems ran slowly and could not keep pace with the quick, flexible systems the Japanese had created.

For example, a Caterpillar plant in East Peoria, Illinois, producing 120 different types of transmissions, tailored and assembled transmission cases at 35 different stations along the production line, each requiring a skilled operator. Each station could handle only one type of case at a time, which resulted in batch processing. While the line made one type of case, all the other types accumulated near the assembly line in a virtual bottleneck. Once operators finished one batch of cases, they had to retool their station for the next batch. The retooling usually took from four hours to two days. In the meantime, more cases piled up. Great inefficiencies also arose from each operator's station as he or she made the necessary ongoing adjustments to get the operation right. This sort of backward technology led to three disastrous years for Caterpillar in the mid-1980s as it fell victim to competition from Japanese rivals.

❧ The Key Question

How do you get an organizational culture to embrace new technology?

Caterpillar's Answer

Unwilling to watch the company get eaten alive by its competitors, Caterpillar executives turned their attention to introducing new technology. In 1986, Caterpillar began an enormous capital improvement program called "Plant With A Future" (PWAF), designed to upgrade all plants and operations in order to eliminate rampant inefficiency. By the end of the 1980s, Caterpillar's tab had run up to $2 billion, an investment the company estimated would bring savings of up to $1.5 billion per year beginning in 1991.

At the transmission plant, for example, 4 new work stations, each computerized and capable of assembling transmission cases on its own, stand where the old line with 35 stations stood. These 4 work stations will eventually be joined by 28 more, each one able to perform the operations that once required 35 different stations. Manned by a single operator, each of the new robotic work stations can quickly select the right tools for a new type of case and make necessary adjustments in a matter of seconds.

How does all of this affect the Caterpillar culture? Donald Fites, Caterpillar's new chairman of the board, has moved engineering, design, marketing, and pricing personnel into the plant locations, so that everyone dealing with a family of products can work together to build the same kind of culture around customer needs and new technology. Fites believes that Caterpillar's strong culture has eagerly embraced the new technology. Even marketing and distribution people who were once far removed from the manufacturing side of the business can coordinate within product teams to better serve their customers. Caterpillar executives wisely tied the new manufacturing technology into an opportunity to more quickly and effectively respond to customer needs for product and service, already an ingrained cultural value among Caterpillar employees. The new technology was never a threat but an enhancement to the organization's culture.

Suggested Right Answers

To help an existing culture embrace new technology, consider the following:

1. *Remove the fear and resistance from your people by clearly communicating that you will retrain them, not lay them off, as the new technology comes on board.*

2. *If embracing new technology does entail layoffs, make sure you do so quickly, then create a stable environment for the new technology.*

3. *Don't make the mistake of thinking or saying that new technology will solve all your problems.*

4. *Make sure new technology compliments, enhances, or supports the existing, important values of your organizational culture.*

5. *As you invest in new technology and introduce it to your culture, carefully evaluate, modify, or upgrade it.*

6. *Always praise your people as much as you praise your technology for cost reductions or margin improvements.*

Applying Right Answers

The book-publishing industry has been surprisingly slow to embrace technology. For many companies—even the biggest—the production process has changed little since Gutenberg. But the wheels of progress do move forward, and a few publishing companies have begun applying high-tech methods to crank out books much faster than they ever could before.

An executive editor for a medium-sized publishing company in New York City (I'll call him Bob) was keenly interested in new approaches to book design, typesetting, and proofreading, but, unfortunately, his 175-year-old firm did not take to new technology gracefully. Pressed by authors and agents to capitalize on disk-based manuscripts that could cut production time from 12 months to 3 months, Bob decided that only by creating such a capability outside the company's main culture could he demonstrate the benefits to senior management and other editors.

The head of the company gave Bob permission to take five manuscripts scheduled for publication in the upcoming season and put them on another track outside the company, as a test case. From beginning to end, these projects followed a high-tech path, with authors using word processors to generate their manuscripts and turning over production disks rather than hard copy. Those disks drove the typesetting equipment, and their output required much less proofreading. Both authors and editors made changes in the manuscripts on computers, reducing the flow of paper and saving a lot of turnaround time. The five books came out with fewer mistakes in half the usual time, giving Bob the case he needed to convince senior management and the company's production people that new technology could bring great benefits. He also took steps to show the production people how their increased efficiency could allow them to focus on additional projects and increase overall output. The success of Bob's approach proved the wisdom of his former writing teacher's maxim, "Show, don't tell."

38

Are You Behind or Ahead of the Technology Wave?

ૐ

*H*as something like this ever happened to you? A small manufacturing firm decided to purchase an expensive plastic extruder that was supposed to speed up its production process and greatly enhance both productivity and quality. Since the machine's cost had decimated the company's capital budget, the CEO was fit to be tied when a visiting customer pointed out that this particular piece of equipment was already outdated. How did the customer know this? He'd attended a specialized technology trade show six months earlier. Since no one from the small manufacturing company had gone to that show, the company decision makers relied upon the salesman who sold them the piece of equipment to keep them ahead of the technology wave. Unfortunately, that approach had put them well behind it.

Smith-Corona fell behind the wave, too, and as early as a decade ago, Smith-Corona executives detected a decline in the market for electronic typewriters. Consequently, the company began to throw its efforts into the word-processing machines that were clearly the wave of the future. Unfortunately, the company didn't take into account the even bigger wave of personal computers about to overwhelm the market. In the past 10 years, personal computers with word-processing programs have not only made electronic typewriters candidates for inclusion in a Smithsonian exhibit but have also outpaced and outperformed word-processing machines. While Smith-Corona has developed quite efficient word-processing machines, it just hasn't been able to compete effectively for the consumer's dollar. Ironically for Smith-Corona, operating on the leading edge of one technology wave put it far behind another wave. Nevertheless, Smith-Corona executives claim they have staked out a strong niche for their products, one they can maintain and service better than any other manufacturer in the field.

‌ *The Key Question*

How do you assess your real position with regard to various waves of technology?

Smith-Corona's Answer

While Smith-Corona executives continue to express optimism about maintaining their position in the word-processing niche, the results don't seem to support their view. Profits have sagged so much—some analysts predicted as much as a 40 percent slide in the early 1990s. As personal computer prices continue to fall, coming perilously close to those for Smith-Corona's word processors, Smith-Corona will find its niche becoming more and more squeezed. Retailers are already riding the personal computer wave. To make matters worse, Smith-Corona, previously a subsidiary of the British conglomerate Hanson TLC, recently went public in a move that upset many investors. Smith-Corona's stock has plummeted, and the prospects for a climb back look bleak. Smith-Corona, it seems, was looking at the wrong technology wave.

Suggested Right Answers

The following points should help you pinpoint your own company's position with respect to a particular technology wave:

1. *Always consider technology waves in terms of a long-term horizon, (i.e., 10 to 20 years).*

2. *Be mindful that just because you are ahead of one technology wave does not mean you are ahead of a larger, more profound one.*

3. *Expect technological change to move at an accelerated clip in the future.*

4. *During times of great technological uncertainty, you might want to remain slightly behind the leading edge of a particular wave in order to avoid unnecessary risk and be well positioned to marshal your resources when the preferred technology emerges.*

5. *No matter what your industry, and no matter what your technology, new waves will inevitably make even the most current technology obsolete.*

Applying Right Answers

The newly appointed CEO of a midsized Southeastern paint manufacturing company (I'll call him Syd) was charged with helping the company effect the transition from a midsized, family-run operation to a large, professionally managed conglomerate. Early on, Syd looked closely at the warehousing of paint products and materials because he believed that streamlining and modernizing that function would improve service, reduce costs, and create a model for the industry. After consulting with three different engineering firms on the design of a state-of-the-art warehousing system, Syd finally decided to work with the one that seemed most forward thinking.

One year and $10 million later, Syd held an open house, inviting customers and dealers to tour the new facility. Since the event captured the attention of the local media, Syd felt certain he'd made the right move. Several articles appeared in the business press, and a local television station ran a full 10-minute segment on the evening news. Everyone marveled at this new warehousing system that was so sophisticated that it could even mix paint automatically. How marvelous to see a once stodgy old company race to the leading edge of technology.

A mere week later, however, calamity struck when Syd discovered that the warehousing facility just didn't work. Over the next several weeks, a million problems cropped up as the company attempted to put the warehouse into full operation. Paint-mixing mistakes, miscued orders, and breakdowns in retrieval gear became so frequent that Syd soon had to close down the new warehouse. The debacle cost Syd his job. Some people make the mistake of riding the wrong technology wave, but Syd made the mistake of riding one that wasn't even there.

39

Does Technology Empower You?

When I first got the latest version of a new desktop publishing program, PageMaker, for my Macintosh, I was excited about all the design and graphics power now at my disposal. Shortly thereafter, I found myself working a set of charts into the text of a management report, and I became so enamored with designing these charts and exploring PageMaker's possibilities that I ended up with 10 different versions of everything. Some time later, I sat back and said to myself, "Hold it. This program is supposed to save me time, but I've wasted several hours!" It's so easy to get enamored of new technology that it distracts us from the real task at hand. At that point, technology entertains, but doesn't empower.

Johnson Controls, a producer of systems and controls for regulating home and workplace temperatures, recently shifted some of its attention to the issue of empowering technology. With its new METASYS Facilities Management System, for example, Johnson Controls makes it easier for technicians to zero in on and correct problems. In essence, this approach decentralizes the computer control system.

Most large office and commercial buildings employ a central computer that controls everything from heating and cooling to fire safety, lighting, and security. When a problem occurs in one of these areas, it may take hours or even days for building engineers to isolate the problem as they chase back and forth from one location to another by "trial and error." Johnson Controls's new system allows a building engineer to tap into the computer with a hand-held terminal so that he or she can monitor the operation of the system, locate problems, and then make necessary adjustments. Johnson Controls's customers have heralded the META-SYS Facilities Management System as a technology improvement that really does empower its users.

⁊ *The Key Question*

How do you determine whether or not technology empowers your people?

Johnson Controls's Answer

Johnson Controls wanted to empower two kinds of people with METASYS. One group consisted of the company's own service personnel who constantly complained about the difficulties they encountered isolating problems in systems they had installed. The other group consisted of the building engineers who actually maintained the customers' office buildings. This latter group also desired ways to improve their effectiveness at correcting problems in ever more complex systems. Johnson Controls's executives, heeding both requests, came up with a truly empowering technology, one that a building engineer for a skyscraper in New York City called the greatest productivity breakthrough in 20 years.

Not only does the new system empower engineers, it also empowers tenants by removing the distractions and disruptions often caused by building maintenance problems. Johnson Controls's new system also saves a lot of money. At some sites, it has cut operating costs as much as 30 percent per year. While the new system bears a high price tag, approximately $700,000 for a large office building, it promises to pay for itself quickly through productivity gains, cost savings, and tenant satisfaction.

Suggested Right Answers

To ensure that technology truly empowers people, make sure it accomplishes one or more of the following:

1. *Saves time.*

2. *Saves money.*

3. *Enhances quality.*

4. *Improves service.*

5. *Gives you a competitive advantage.*

6. *Better utilizes talent.*

7. *Motivates usage.*

8. *Increases customer satisfaction.*

Applying Right Answers

A large electric utility company was looking for more efficient and effective ways to read its meters. The old system, which involved meter readers logging data collected from homes or other buildings into a notebook and then taking that notebook to the office for input into a computer, was extremely time consuming and costly. When the department head in charge of meter reading (I'll call him Bill) learned about a new meter-reading system that had just come on the market, he thought he may have found the answer to his company's needs. The new system involved the use of a hand-held calculator that allowed meter readers to punch in meter readings that could eventually be dumped into the main office's central computer. The projected savings, according to the sales representative, could reach 30 percent in terms of labor productivity and 40 percent in terms of data transfer.

Completely sold on the new system, Bill believed it would empower his meter readers to accomplish a lot more work in less time, making it possible for some personnel to move to other departments and for the MIS staff to pursue other worthwhile projects. Wisely, Bill decided to experiment with the new program, implementing it on only a fraction of his people's routes to see how it worked. To his consternation, the experiment turned into a complete disaster. Since the hand-held devices could not verify the data a meter reader punched into the unit, many more than the usual number of input mistakes occurred. In addition, the hand-held units did not transfer data to the central computer very accurately. Some irate customers were complaining about the resultant billing inaccuracies. Eventually, all the meter readers had to go back and read everything a second time.

Given the problems with the system, many meter readers began their own backup system, punching the meter data into the hand-held device as well as logging it into their old record books. Ironically, this led to an increase in the time it took meter readers to do their jobs and an increase in the management information staff time required to transfer data, ensure its accuracy, and print out the necessary information. The salesman who had presented the program to Bill and assisted in its implementation assured Bill that they could work out these bugs easily, but Bill cancelled the new meter-reading program after its initial experiment, telling the sales rep to make sure he had squashed all the bugs before darkening his doorstep again.

40

Can You Evaluate the Worth of Your Technology Edge?

~a

A while back, I was so impressed with the ads for a newly developed electric razor that I went right out and bought one, believing that this more expensive model would really provide a technology edge in the form of a closer shave. When I used it, however, I couldn't see any difference between the technologically new version and my old one. How much was the supposed new technology edge worth to me? Not much. So why replace the old one and why pay double the price? If you really do possess a technology edge in your organization, you should be able to calculate its bottom-line results. If you can't, your technology edge may be worthless.

After the breakup of AT&T several years ago, many people believed that the remaining long-distance company would become IBM's major competitor in the computer market. But it just hasn't turned out that way because the new AT&T hasn't yet created the necessary technology edge in its data systems division. AT&T's UNIX, basic software licensed to dozens of computer makers, turned out not to hold a significant advantage, nor did the company's 3B line of minicomputers. The 3B line, which actually originated as telephone switches, never caught on in business applications. AT&T's hoped-for technology edge, it turned out, was largely imaginary and, as a result, AT&T's data systems group racked up a six-year losing streak that hit $1 billion in one year.

❧ The Key Question

What do you do if your technology edge doesn't produce results?

AT&T's Answer

Robert Cavner, head of AT&T's data systems group, quickly recognized the limited worth of AT&T's supposed technology edge and quickly began looking for another. A former Coopers & Lybrand partner, Cavner did not succumb to the illusion of his company's potential competitive advantage in the computer market. Instead, he entered into partnerships with other hardware and software manufacturers while preparing to set up UNIX software as a separate operation owned by a variety of computer companies. To his mind, the real advantage lay in selling systems incorporating a variety of hardware, software, and communication devices. AT&T, he felt, could better establish an edge as a systems integrator, a seller of flexible solutions to information problems.

Cavner's shift in focus has allowed AT&T to focus on distributor network computing and to become the leader in linking heterogenous hardware, achievements that have honed a genuinely sharp edge in the market. The company's claim that they can link diverse equipment better than anyone in the industry has started to work, with the company landing computer orders from American Airlines, Firestone, Pizza Hut, Chrysler, UPS, and the U.S. Transportation Department, business that could generate as much as $850 million over the next few years.

Suggested Right Answers

As you evaluate the results of your technology edge:

1. *Don't assume that a technology edge in one area will easily translate to another area.*

2. *Never expect general technological expertise to automatically create a technology edge that produces bottom-line results.*

3. *Remember that the largest financial investment does not always create the greatest technology edge.*

4. *Constantly evaluate your technology edge for results.*

5. *Take care not to throw away a technology edge prematurely just because you can't find an immediate application that makes money.*

Applying Right Answers

A brilliant physicist (I'll call him Henry) had spent several years working for NASA before starting a company that designed precision sensing equipment and devices. The idea for his company came to him when NASA was searching for a contractor to improve the sensing capabilities of one of its satellite probes and could not find an appropriate supplier. His own successful bid for the contract launched Henry into producing instruments for a number of NASA and Department of Defense applications.

Over the years, Henry's small company grew to employ 50 people, but sales fluctuated wildly from $1 million to $6 million from year to year. The company had developed a number of technological advancements, including a new motion-sensing device that could detect the slightest movement of a small object at an amazing distance. Given what seemed like unlimited commercial applications for this technology, Henry decided to jump into mass marketing. After developing a prototype security alarm system based on the new movement-sensing process, Henry's firm marketed it aggressively to security system manufacturers, but to Henry's astonishment, no one seemed interested. Several hundred thousand dollars later, Henry sold the rights to the technology to another small company. Since no mass-market applications had materialized, the sale of the technology would at least allow him to defray some of his R&D and marketing costs.

Less than 18 months later, the company to which Henry had sold his technology developed an application of the technology for manufacturers requiring more precise reaction to movement along sophisticated assembly and processing lines. In the next five years, that company accumulated more than $200 million in sales, with the promise of even more in other arenas. Henry's business still fluctuates between $1 million and $6 million a year, depending on government contracts, but Henry has also entered into three joint ventures with other firms that could effectively apply his technological developments to other opportunities. Two of the joint ventures have racked up strong sales and profits. Henry learned the hard way that creating a technology edge is only the first step, then you must successfully apply it to get bottom-line results.

Part IX

ALLIANCES

41

Do You Know How to Locate New Allies?

———— ❧ ————

While looking for a video pro-
duction company that would be willing to joint-venture an am-
bitious training series with me, I searched high and low in
California and New York, all to no avail. Then one day I found
myself sitting in the dentist's chair, and although I had known
the man for a number of years, I never knew until I told him my
problem that day that he owned a video production company that
he ran on the side. Having turned out some top-quality work,
the company was looking for projects just like mine. Leaving my
friend's office that day, I thought how we often overlook potential
strategic alliances that are sitting right under our noses.

In the waste-to-energy business, Ogden Projects, an 89 percent
owned subsidiary of Ogden Corporation, didn't make that mistake. Ogden Projects specializes in building and operating high-
technology incinerators that turn garbage into electricity. Competitors such as Wheelabrator do the same thing but not the same
way Ogden does it. Knowing the value of solid alliances, Ogden
enters into long-term contractual agreements (20 to 25 years) with
municipalities to build and operate waste-to-energy plants for a
fixed operating fee that fluctuates with the Consumer Price Index.
In contrast, Ogden's competitors strategically locate their plants
to serve the open market. Such open market plants accept garbage

at the market rate of $40 to $80 a ton. When they can command a high price, these plants do well, but when they can't, they struggle. Ogden typically agrees to a price around $60 a ton, giving them their required 30 percent return on equity and a constant, predictable cash flow. Also, because Ogden enters into a contractual arrangement with a local community, environmental issues don't become project stoppers. Support for a plant comes a lot easier when the municipality itself wants to build it.

Its unique alliances have allowed Ogden to bypass Wheelabrator, the old market leader, and gain 20 percent of the national waste-to-energy market, the largest share held by any one company. Ogden's earnings have grown over 300 percent in the past year to over $20 million. The company operates 13 plants, with plans to open 7 more by 1995.

The Key Question

Where can you find new alliances?

Ogden's Answer

Early on, Ogden looked to its customers—local governments and communities—for alliances. David Sokol, CEO of Ogden Projects and architect of the company's alliances with municipalities, chose a low-risk strategic direction that eventually produced the company's major strategic advantage. Sokol's tenacity and ingenuity helped him find potential alliances right under Ogden's nose, with its most obvious stakeholders, its customers.

Ogden did it first and now; its competitors are following suit. Even Wheelabrator, once the industry leader, has begun setting up the same kind of alliances. Fortunately for Ogden, doing it first has put it far ahead of the pack, with a steady stream of 25-year guaranteed earnings.

Suggested Right Answers

When looking for potential allies to strengthen your strategic direction, follow these steps:

1. **Begin by looking for potential allies among competitors, suppliers, substitute product/service providers, new entrants, and buyers.**

2. **Consider all of your organization's stakeholders as potential sources for formal or informal alliances.**

3. **Pay close attention to the kinds of partnerships, joint-ventures, mergers, acquisitions, affiliations, and alliances taking place in all sectors of the economy, and consider doing something similar.**

Applying Right Answers

The newly appointed junior partner of a 100-person information consulting firm (I'll call him Stern) probably should have left the issue of strategic alliances to his senior partners, but if he had, the firm would have missed out on a fabulous opportunity for growth and development.

Stern has always been preoccupied with alliances. Wherever he's worked, he's seen competitors, suppliers, shareholders, new companies coming into the market, and customers as potential partners, and he has constantly pored through the business media to identify new kinds of partnerships in every industry imaginable. Over the years, he often came back to the notion that other firms in the marketplace offering services not directly competing with his own firm's could make ideal matches, an idea he fervently wanted to apply to his new firm. The company often sought help from three sources when developing a new information system for a client: the vendor of the equipment, a strategic management consulting firm, and an information systems implementation firm.

While each of these different sources claimed it could design and implement a complete information system, everyone in the industry agreed that each possessed strengths and limitations about which customers were seldom fully aware. Thus, clients usually found themselves somewhat at the mercy of salesmanship.

Why not band these four types of companies together to provide an optimum service for the customer and growth opportunities for the partners? To answer that question, Stern obtained permission from a senior partner to explore the possibilities quietly and cautiously.

First, Stern identified three alliance candidates: a strategic management consulting firm about the same size as his own firm, a vendor that often aided his firm on assignments with customers and a systems integration and implementation firm. To each he made a simple, informal presentation stressing the benefits of an integrated approach. Everyone could win, both partners and customers. Though skeptical at first, each of the potential partners found Stern's ideas intriguing.

After several more detailed discussions with all of the prospects, Stern assembled a detailed proposal for the senior partners in his own firm. All he wanted was a chance to experiment with the concept on one new customer. "Okay," agreed his superiors, "but whose customer and who would take the lead?" "We'll start the ball rolling," Stern answered, "and we'll go after a plum account neither we nor our new partners have been able to land."

Of course, it was easier said than done, but within six months, Stern had landed the account for the new consortium, beating out several much larger rivals, and the customer couldn't have been more pleased with the results. Its satisfaction led to three referrals with which the alliance secured contracts quite easily. Stern himself became a coordinator of joint activities, overseeing the strategic management firm's initial assessment of the customer's information needs, his own company's design of the new system, the vendor organization's delivery and installation of equipment, and the implementation firm's start-up and monitoring of the new system.

The alliance worked so well that Stern became a senior partner in his own company a year later, having engineered growth far beyond the company's original goal. Although a number of competitors have imitated the program, Stern continues to lead the way as Stern and his allies keep coming up with new and different kinds of alliances that better satisfy customers. His latest idea is to combine a marketing research firm and a consortium of companies designing and implementing customer satisfaction management information systems.

42

Do You Form Long- or Short-Term Alliances?

— ❧ —

When a flood hit our community, thousands of people banded together to protect homes and businesses and to aid those who had suffered the most. Service organizations, church organizations, companies, and individuals from all walks of life formed an alliance to meet this crisis. But when the crisis passed, the alliance dissolved, along with the power of unity we had all felt.

The same thing happens all the time in the corporate world. Companies form alliances through mergers, acquisitions, joint ventures, or partnerships to meet the needs of the moment, to address a crisis, to take advantage of certain short-term opportunities, or simply for convenience' sake. Then, as in our community, those alliances can fade quickly if they cease paying dividends. How much would we all benefit if our communities and corporations maintained their alliances over longer periods of time?

For example, take the cement industry in the United States, which has been declining for several years. Many U.S. cement companies have looked for alliances with foreign companies to survive the shake-out and create profitable, worldwide organizations. One of them, Lone Star, once the healthiest and largest domestic U.S. cement maker, embarked on just such a search after its industry began suffering from excess capacity and low prices. Unfortunately, Lone Star seemed only interested in short-term gains, as its CEO, James Stewart, exploited his company's alliances simply as a means of selling assets, creating cash, and maintaining short-term profitability. When the dust settled, Lone Star had sold off 50 percent of many of its companies to British, Japanese, and Swiss buyers.

While Lone Star's moves initially seemed to benefit the company, with many analysts convinced that Stewart was beginning to position the company as a worldwide force in the cement industry, its loss of a long list of assets and vital portions of itself eventually took its toll. Since 1986, sales and earnings have dropped a whopping 50 percent.

❧ The Key Question

How do you avoid short-term alliances that can damage long-term growth and development?

Lone Star's Answer

If Lone Star had really invested in its alliances with British, Swiss, and Japanese companies, its current situation might look dramatically different. Unfortunately, the pattern of short-term alliances to boost profits has drained Lone Star of much of its money-making capability. Stewart, overly enamored with deal making, incurred all of the costs of arranging such deals but never structured or managed them to produce long-term benefit. Consequently, James Stewart has simply managed to divest Lone Star of its best cement-making assets. In the last four years alone, the company has unloaded $600 million of assets. If Lone Star executives had adopted a more patient perspective on their international alliances, the company would not likely sit in such a sorry position today.

Suggested Right Answers

In order to avoid short-term alliances that may damage the long-term well-being of your organization, you should look for partners that match your own vision and values in the following areas:

1. *Expectations for growth, development, and pay-off.*

2. *Motivation for entering the alliance.*

3. *Purpose of the alliance.*

4. *Long-range viability of the alliance.*

Applying Right Answers

A senior partner with a major accounting firm (I'll call him Earl) was responsible for looking for alliances with software development companies with which his firm could develop financial systems software that would support its consulting and accounting services. Earl's first alliance involved a small, but growing, software development company that emphasized four different types of applications: financial, medical, legal, and engineering. Concluding that this company's capabilities could support a long-term relationship, Earl convinced its owners to devote the majority of their efforts to financial systems software.

At first the president of the software development company (I'll call him Sutton) had hesitated putting all of his eggs in the financial systems basket. Was his potential partner really committed to making this alliance work in the long term? After a series of discussions, Earl managed to convince Sutton that his firm really would support the relationship far into the future, and Sutton's company began to shift its emphasis away from all non-financial applications, until its financial systems work comprised over 75 percent of its activities. In the meantime, Earl, always alert for additional alliances, had entered into an agreement with another software development firm, one that already concentrated on financial systems programs and was riding on a faster growth track than Sutton's company. Its new program for integrating business planning, financial planning, and reporting was receiving rave reviews from every corner of the industry. Before long, the firm began to focus on the other software company, leaving Sutton's outfit languishing for a lack of necessary resources and attention. Though Sutton's company was working on two very promising programs, at least a year would elapse before they could be marketed. In light of that, the accounting firm sent promised development dollars elsewhere.

The growing mismatch between the two companies' motivations and expectations resulted in a breakup and a lawsuit by Sutton against his former partner for misrepresentation of corporate commitments. The firm filed a countersuit against Sutton, making it impossible for him to sell any of his financial systems software to anyone else until the differences between the two companies were ironed out.

It took two years to resolve the situation in an out-of-court settlement which required Sutton to turn over one of his programs to the firm for their exclusive use in return for $150,000 in cash. To Sutton's everlasting regret, the misguided alliance had set his company five years behind its long-term objectives. He lamented recently, "I'll never enter into another alliance with anyone. Period." And that's too bad, because his industry tends to depend on such partnerships more than most.

43

When Should You Change Alliances?

~~~~~~~~~~ ❧ ~~~~~~~~~~

Divorce visits hardships on every member of a family, particularly for children, but in some cases, parents staying together "for the sake of the children" can also create serious problems. In other cases, parents working out their difficulties "for the sake of the children" have strengthened their lives and their relationships. How do parents make such difficult choices? Usually, it's the inequality of commitment, desire, effort, or fidelity that drives divorce. One or both of the partners begins to make choices that undermine the marriage. Such choices must be changed or altered if the marriage is to last. The same holds true for organizations when they choose to continue or abandon an alliance; even when the level of financial investment differs, an inequality of commitment, desire, effort, and fidelity among alliance partners can spell disaster unless effectively addressed and corrected.

Pioneer, the Japanese electronics company, is best known for its stereo and radio equipment, but in the late 1970s, the company was experimenting with a laser video technology that seemed to offer great promise. By 1980, Pioneer had entered into a joint venture with IBM and MCA, with Pioneer bringing electronics experience to the venture, IBM sophisticated computer expertise, and MCA strong movie-making and music-recording abilities.

This seemingly wonderful alliance promised to make laser videos a viable product for the 1980s. Unfortunately, the marriage did not unfold as its partners envisioned. While Pioneer had fully committed its best resources to the technology, MCA was using an old record factory to make the laser disks, many of which did not perform well. When customers who bought the new laser disk players expressed disappointment in quality, suddenly the once bright three-way alliance turned sour. In 1982, IBM and MCA gave up on the project, and Pioneer purchased the player and disk manufacturing plants in the United States. IBM and MCA, glad to get out of the deal, fully expected Pioneer to lose a lot of money betting on a technology that simply wasn't going to succeed. To their way of thinking, videotape would continue to dominate the business for the decades to come. As for Pioneer, it also wanted out of an alliance with recalcitrant partners, figuring that if it was ever going to succeed with laser disk technology, it would have to do so on its own.

ᐛ The Key Question

How do you decide whether you should retain or end an alliance?

Pioneer's Answer

From Pioneer's perspective, the company had already invested five years in the development of the laser video technology and saw no reason to quit. Since MCA's quality problems had hurt the cause, Pioneer concluded that it should end the alliance with MCA. While IBM still contributed to the effort, the unattractive picture for the future of video disks caused its attention to the joint venture with Pioneer to wane. Both IBM and MCA saw better places to put their time and money.

After Pioneer bought out its partners, it spent millions of dollars to improve the antiquated record factory by installing sorely needed sterile rooms and sophisticated production systems. Then, for the next eight years, Pioneer nursed along the laser disk technology, making steady improvements on a product that could provide higher-quality picture resolution and superior audio sound.

The investment finally paid off in 1990, when 1.2 million Japanese consumers paid $600 each for Pioneer's video disk systems. In the same year, over 200,000 Americans purchased video disk players, and that's just the beginning. In a market now growing at a rate of 35 percent annually, Pioneer controls 75 percent of the action. The Pioneer technology has become the standard of the industry as Panasonic, Sony, and others have imitated it. By the year 1994, Pioneer expects to be selling $4 billion worth of laser disk players annually. That doesn't count disk sales, which Pioneer expects to grow at an even faster rate than the video disk-player market. Pioneer makes 90 percent of the disks produced in the U.S.

The 13-year Pioneer investment has turned out to be a brilliant move, making the company's future very bright indeed. As for the alliance with IBM and MCA, Pioneer chose to go down the road by itself because its partners lacked the vision and commitment to continue. Today, IBM and MCA may wish they'd kept the marriage alive.

Suggested Right Answers

Whenever external or internal changes affect an alliance, ask yourself:

1. *Does the alliance still make sense?*

2. *Does the alliance need a new set of timetables, expectations, and commitments?*

3. *Are any of the partners compromising the future success of the project or joint venture?*

4. *Has the balance of equal and mutual interest shifted?*

5. *Have the priorities and purposes of the alliance significantly changed?*

6. *Do any of the partners want out of the alliance, and if so, why?*

7. *Do any of the partners want to buy out the other partners, and if so, why?*

8. *Will further changes make the picture brighter or bleaker?*

Applying Right Answers

A hotel chain and an amusement park company entered into a joint venture to develop a major resort and recreation park in Florida, and the two companies each made an initial investment of $1 million over an 18-month period. Having selected a site, drawn up architectural plans, and purchased an option on the property, the alliance obtained all the necessary approvals for construction and completed all the requisite legal work and financial projections. It was time to break ground. However, as the two companies were preparing to begin construction in early spring, a sinkhole developed in the center of the property, raising serious questions about the safety and viability of the project. After a month of study, the partners concluded that they could solve the sinkhole problem with landfill and excavation and proceeded to spend several hundred thousand dollars filling in the sinkhole to make sure that they were building on geologically firm ground. Just as they had finished dealing with the first sinkhole, however, another appeared on the property. At this point, the chief financial officer for the hotel chain (I'll call him Erik) conducted a new financial analysis of the joint venture in the context of spending several hundred thousand dollars more to correct the second sinkhole, and the possibility of needing to allocate another

$2 million for a contingency fund to cover the costs of additional sinkholes. Those eventualities also entailed delaying actual construction another several months.

During the analysis, Erik discovered that if the partners had allowed for these costs at the outset, they probably would not have entered into the alliance. When he presented his findings to the managements of both companies, both groups called for a temporary halt to the project. After the meeting, the president of the hotel chain asked Erik what he thought they should do, and Erik argued that since almost $3.5 million had already been expended, the only way to recoup that money was to move forward with the project. After much deliberation, the presidents of the hotel chain and the amusement park company agreed with Erik, and work proceeded.

The following spring, after construction had started on the resort hotel and several recreational facilities, a third sinkhole developed. This turn of events prompted the state agency responsible for overseeing such development to withdraw its approval until completion of a new geological study. Unfortunately, the new study concluded that enough uncertainty surrounded the property that construction should be postponed indefinitely. By this time, the two companies had sunk over $5 million into the project and were faced with the prospect of waiting another year or two before construction could resume. In a fit of anger, the president of the hotel chain fired Erik for his poor judgment and abruptly cancelled his company's involvement in the undertaking. The property was sold two years later at a drastically reduced price to another resort developer, who ultimately solved the sinkhole problem and built the same recreational and resort facility the two original partners had envisioned. Today, that resort is operating and producing an attractive profit.

Sometimes, alliances make business decisions more difficult, but they can also enhance business success if the right decisions are made when circumstances surrounding an alliance change.

44

Do Your Alliances Make Sense to Everyone Involved?

— ❧ —

When two school districts recently combined, parents immediately rebelled. Not understanding the rationale behind the combination, they vigorously circulated petitions and flocked to the superintendent's office to protest. For a full year, this issue virtually gridlocked the community. Eventually, however, the reasons for the combination, all aimed at improving the quality of education, became clear to residents, and many of the initial fears subsided. Unfortunately, it took almost two years and a lot of wasted energy and emotion to calm the community down. All too often, organizations go through the same turmoil when they enter into alliances that do not on the surface make sense to everyone involved. In such instances, an organization, like our communities, can gridlock for months or even years.

Federal Express recently made several moves to transform itself into one of the world's largest and most permanent players in the package/delivery market. In 1984, company officials drafted a document, several hundred pages long, detailing specific goals and strategies for every aspect of the company, all aimed at creating a fully global Federal Express by the year 2000. Fed Ex chairman, Fred Smith, believing that any carrier that wanted to survive in the twenty-first century must offer worldwide service, knew also that any mergers, acquisitions, and alliances that the company undertook must make sense to every Federal Express employee.

Since 1984, Federal Express has taken several concrete steps to implement its globalization strategy. In one of the company's boldest moves, it acquired the Flying Tigers carrier and the parent company, Tiger International. Flying Tigers, already an international presence, gave Federal Express instant access to delivery routes in Asia, South America, Australia, and Europe. In addition to that acquisition, Federal Express began putting together massive ground networks throughout Europe, preparing for 1992 when a united European market will further tap Federal Express's overnight delivery capabilities. The establishment of such ground networks has required a number of strategic alliances with governments, communities, and businesses throughout Europe.

❧ The Key Question

How do you make sure that your organization's alliances make sense to everyone within the organization?

Federal Express's Answer

Fred Smith has been preparing his people for many years to become part of the largest and best transportation company in the world. He painstakingly presents and discusses his plans for entering into the necessary worldwide alliances with everyone connected to the Federal Express system. The sharing of this information, and the inclusion of Federal Express employees in the process of making it happen, has made a big difference.

Integrating the Tiger International acquisition will not be easy for Federal Express because Tiger has focused on heavier packages and cargo than Federal Express. It also employs 65,000 workers who belong to a union, and services several customers, like UPS, which compete with Federal Express. Overcoming these challenges won't happen without difficulties, but Fred Smith has taken care to ensure that his people believe that the Federal Express/Tiger International linkup makes sense. He has also made sure the ground network in Europe, a very expensive proposition, also makes sense to the company's thousands of employees, and has thus encouraged them to make the best possible ground networking decisions and related government, community, and business alliances. Fred Smith instinctively knew that it would take everyone pulling together to make such alliances and globalization work. If you ask any Federal Express employee, he or she will quickly tell you that globalization is Federal Express's destiny. That type of grassroots commitment, more than anything else, taps the full potential of any alliance.

Suggested Right Answers

You may want to take the following steps prior to entering into any strategic alliance in order to make sure that when it comes about, it makes sense to everyone involved:

1. *Take care that everyone in the organization understands that alliances lie on the horizon.*

2. *Communicate with people throughout the organization about the kinds of alliances that may make the most sense for your organization.*

3. *Make sure that everyone involved in the strategic and business planning processes look for alliances that make the most sense for the organization.*

4. *Tie the discussion of alliances or prospective alliances into the overall picture of the organization's future.*

5. *When you are considering a potential alliance, don't be afraid to ask your people what they think, even if you must disguise*

the name of the target company and generalize the specifics to protect confidentiality.

6. *If you discover a potential alliance that has not been adequately presented to your people, communicate as much as you can, as quickly as you can, to avoid the wasted resources and productivity slumps that always attend alliances that don't make sense to everyone.*

Applying Right Answers

While working for a large furniture manufacturer in North Carolina, a young marketing executive I'll call Isaac had been developing a strong network of manufacturers' representatives throughout North America over the last five years. Reporting to the vice president of Marketing, he had received a clear mandate to create the strongest manufacturers' rep organization in the industry. Isaac had put his heart and soul into the effort and after five years had achieved his objective with over 60 reps throughout North America.

Then one day, while on vacation on the Yucatan Peninsula, Isaac called the office and was startled by the news that his company was entering into a long-term partnership with a well-known housewares and home accessories manufacturer. What shocked Isaac most was a press release his secretary read to him that announced the sharing of marketing and sales functions with the new partner. Since the housewares and accessories company fielded its own highly visible sales force, Isaac couldn't imagine how that sales force would dovetail with the manufacturers' rep organization he had built. He immediately called his boss for clarification. Unfortunately, his boss, almost as much in the dark as Isaac, couldn't provide much assurance that the plan made sense.

Needless to say, the news not only ruined Isaac's vacation, but in the weeks after his return, it made his life miserable. The more questions he asked, the fewer answers he heard. His own reps were beginning to lose faith in him and the company. Eventually, management hired a consulting firm to study the issue and make recommendations about achieving synergy between the two companies. During the ensuing weeks and months, Isaac's productivity reached an all-time low as 22 of the manufacturers' reps he had worked so hard to bring into the company quit in disgust. Finally, four months later, the consulting firm returned with its recommendations, suggesting that both the housewares sales force and the manufacturers' reps should remain in place servicing separate accounts. Isaac couldn't quite believe in the consultant's recommendations because he, like everyone else, had assumed that his manufacturers' reps would be supplanted by the sales force of the other company. He feared that the lost productivity and lost sales could never be recovered and would forever cast a cloud over the two companies in the minds of the manufacturers' reps.

Gradually, however, in the months afterward, the alliance did begin to make more sense to Isaac and everyone else. Even some of the manufacturers' reps began to discard their anxiety and build new commitment to the combined effort. Still, Isaac felt that an awful lot of grief, inefficiency, and ineffectiveness that could have been avoided if only the senior managements of the two companies had better prepared people for the alliance. In retrospect, the recommendations from the consulting firm were really quite predictable, but everyone was just so upset no one could make sense of it all.

45

Have Alliances Increased Your Competitiveness?

❧

---

*H*aving to separate from a business partner and friend not long ago was one of the most difficult things I have ever done, even though everyone concerned agreed that our relationship was holding both of us back and compromising the progress of our consulting firm. My partner had grown overly dependent upon me, and I, in turn, expected too much from him. Basically, my inability to provide the ongoing concrete support he needed made it difficult for him to apply his talents and expertise, and the gap between us did nothing but widen. Finally, that gulf resulted in our going our separate ways. Good alliances promote the well-being of all partners, and when they don't, they shouldn't be maintained, despite whatever mutual respect and admiration may exist.

While Apple Computer rang up astonishing success early in its development, the company has not fared so well recently in Japan, where in 1989 it carried a tiny 1.4 percent of the personal computer market. Both American and Japanese investigations into the cause of Apple's failure in Japan have agreed that the fault lies with Apple management, which has in the past failed to forge the alliances necessary for doing business the Japanese way. Apple has preferred playing the lone wolf in a market where alliances historically increase competitiveness. When NEC, Apple's main

---

competitor in Japan, came out with its personal computer, the company sent managers to all Japanese software houses to build trusting relationships and persuade developers to write programs for NEC PCs. Apple, on the other hand, refusing to build such relationships, quickly developed a reputation for "Yankee arrogance" and became a pariah among Japanese programmers. As a result, only 15 Japanese software packages were developed for the Macintosh, compared to 5000 for NEC, enabling the latter to capture 60 percent of the Japanese PC market. Apple lost additional ground when it declined following the Japanese tradition of paying developers to convert their programs to run on specific computers, refused lending their machines out to programmers, and remained aloof from Japan's largest software trade group, the Japan Personal Computer Software Association. All these moves made Apple an outsider, unable to exploit relationships that could result in sorely needed programs for its machines.

❧ *The Key Question*

How do you make sure your alliances increase competitiveness?

Apple-Japan's Answer

Since 1989, Apple-Japan has aggressively tried to build the necessary alliances in the Japanese market. Having finally realized that competitiveness in Japanese markets hinged on paying attention to strategic alliances, Apple joined the Japan Personal Computer Software Association and other trade groups. This move showed Japanese developers and programmers that Apple was finally willing to play by their rules. In addition, Apple actively recruited Japanese software developers and gave them early access to Apple products so they could prepare programs in a timely fashion. Engineers from U.S. software companies who had created proven software products for Apple Computers crossed the Pacific to forge ties with their Japanese counterparts and co-develop Japanese products based on their successful U.S. programs.

As soon as Apple began to forge alliances with trade groups, programmers, and software developers in Japan, it quickly shed its reputation for "Yankee arrogance." Results came rapidly. Already, Japan's two largest software houses are distributing Macintosh machines and software. Surveys indicate that universities are beginning to prefer Macs and that software writers rank the machines second only to those from NEC. By early 1991, the Mac was starting to make inroads in the graphic arts and publishing fields in Japan, just as it has done in the U.S. Another alliance with Japan's giant publishing house, Iwanami Shoten, resulted in the publication of Japan's first full-length hardcover book via Macintosh technology. Apple CEO John Sculley and everyone else at Apple, it seems, have come to appreciate the competitive value of alliances, especially in tough global markets.

Suggested Right Answers

As you weigh the competitive value of your alliances, consider these points:

1. *Search high and low for possible alliances that can strengthen your own strategy.*

2. *Avoid the pitfall of becoming too inbred and internally focused.*

3. *Remain willing to make certain organizational changes to accommodate an alliance.*

4. *Encourage everyone in the organization to think about potential alliances.*

5. *Develop useful methods for judging the value and performance of an alliance.*

Applying Right Answers

After developing a successful property management firm in the United States, a husband and wife team (I'll call them Ron and Liz) set their sights on expanding into Europe. They had built from scratch a company that managed over 200 different properties, including hotels, office buildings, parks, amusement centers, shopping malls, and apartment complexes. As they began moving into Europe, they linked up with an advertising agency based in London to help launch their campaign. This, they figured, would enable them to communicate their established success with prospective European clients. To do it right would require the marketing and advertising savvy of Europeans, not Americans.

To their surprise, however, this particular alliance did not work out, because although it did gain expertise in European marketing and advertising, it did not increase their actual competitiveness in the European market. Too many other similar property management firms, it turned out, were already vying for the same business. After spending a quarter-million dollars on the campaign, with little concrete success, Ron and Liz decided to search out another kind of alliance, one that really would improve their competitiveness. After a good deal of hard thinking and looking, they selected a real estate development firm involved in developing office complexes, hotels, and apartment buildings in London, Brussels, and Milan. Once they formed that alliance, it didn't take long for the competitive edge to grow sharp. The two firms' abilities made an ideal match, and within months, Ron and Liz were managing 50 properties in Europe, regretting only that they hadn't asked themselves enough tough questions before assuming they'd found the right answer.

Part X

COSTS

46

Can You Define Your Strategic Costs?

———————— ❧ ————————

When my wife and I made some rather large investments a few years ago, we decided to sit down and find ways to cut some of our living costs. Reluctantly, we concluded that we should only eat out once a week, a large cut given our habit of eating out four to six times a week, but an easier one to make than any involving our family's more basic welfare. As we implemented the new plan, my wife and children began to sorely miss going out and the morale of the whole family declined noticeably. After a few weeks of this, my wife and I reconsidered. As we analyzed our earlier decision, we discovered that eating out provided a great opportunity for our family to be together and talk with little distraction. It freed both my wife and me from time-consuming kitchen duty, and it provided a structured getaway from the day's sometimes hectic activities. In the end, we decided that the cost of eating out was a strategic one we should not cut. Similar decisions must be made by organizations, as executives must cut costs during tough times.

In 1985, Nolan Archibald took over at Black & Decker during tough times. In light of the fact that the company was losing a tremendous amount of money, Archibald implemented what he called "a cut and build strategy," one aimed at identifying nonstrategic

———

costs. At the same time, Archibald wanted to define strategic costs that the company should increase in order to grow in the future.

In the ensuing months, Black & Decker closed 5 of 24 plants, laid off 2000 employees, and froze or cut wages of many others. At the same time, Archibald invested millions in product development, marketing, and customer service.

✎ *The Key Question*

How do you decide which costs to cut?

Black & Decker's Answer

Nolan Archibald and his executives at Black & Decker understood the strategic nature of costs. To save their company from decline, they began by identifying which costs did not create a strategic advantage and which ones did. As a result, they tightened the organization's belt without sacrificing new product development, marketing, or customer service. Although having closed 5 of 24 plants by 1986, the company set a goal of introducing 12 new products each year, a goal it has consistently met in an industry where the best firms only introduce 3 or 4 each year. New products introduced between 1986 and 1991 represented approximately 30 percent of Black & Decker's sales. After a $158 million loss in 1985, Black & Decker rebounded to earnings over $100 million on sales of $2.3 billion in the late 1980s. In the early 1990s, 40 percent of Black & Decker sales are coming from new product introductions.

Black & Decker has also spent a lot of time focusing on consumer groups to pinpoint their likes and dislikes, and it has engaged in a lot of market research and "user observation studies" to identify what its customers want. Home use studies and owner surveys help the company determine how to make its products more convenient, more usable, and more versatile. Competitors ridiculed

Black & Decker's new cordless appliances, but the company's attention to what customers really want and need paid off as those cordless appliances did extremely well in the marketplace.

Suggested Right Answers

Keep in mind the following points when you consider cutting costs in your organization:

1. *Determine which costs are strategic and which are not.*

2. *Never cut costs that you identify as strategically important to the long-term viability of your business.*

3. *Do cut nonstrategic costs.*

4. *Always be prepared to increase rather than cut your strategic costs.*

Applying Right Answers

The newly appointed office managing partner in an office of an international business services firm (I'll call him Anton) had received a mandate from the firm's managing partner in New York to turn the office around. Since it had been losing money for the last four years, the firm was actually considering closing it if a turnaround did not occur. With the pressure on, Anton knew that any sort of profit depended on cutting operating costs, and he knew he must effect these cuts quickly in order to keep New York at bay.

After pondering the situation for two months, Anton laid off several professionals and instituted a salary freeze for several others. He also cut professional development budgets for a 12-month period. Though this course of action caused a number of other people to seek employment elsewhere, Anton concluded that their departures would probably benefit the organization in the long run.

During the next several months, it became painfully evident that some of the best and highest-paid people, those with the most promise and competence, had joined the migration, but to balance that fact, the operation did achieve a break-even status and even began to show signs of near-term profitability. As a result, Anton heard nothing but praise from both regional and national officers. Then, six months later, clients began complaining about the level of service in the firm's bookkeeping and legal services. Increased mistakes brought swift heat down upon Anton, especially when the revenues of the office, which Anton had expected to rise further, actually began to drop. Now Anton was wrestling with an even more serious problem—not only were expenses outpacing revenues, but he lacked the professional talent necessary to turn the situation around.

Anton's failure to separate out strategic costs when he launched his cost-cutting spree eventually led to Anton's transfer to a smaller office and the closing of the one he had struggled to revive. In retrospect, some people in New York said that closing the office had been inevitable and that Anton could have done nothing to turn it around, but others, including the managing partner in New York, felt that Anton had taken a wrong-headed approach to the original problem. Whatever the case, Anton's career suffered a jolting setback. He lamented recently, "I just hope I get a chance not to make the same mistake again."

47

What's Your Attitude Toward Costs?

ε**φ**

---

*T*he federal government faces a real dilemma when it comes to cutting costs because across-the-board cuts that might reduce the federal deficit can create disastrous effects in certain sectors of the economy and offend various and sundry interest groups. As a result, no one has ever concocted an effective plan than can cut costs in a more discriminating way, and the federal deficit continues to rise. In the area of cost cutting, the federal government remains fickle, arbitrary, and even destructive, unable to develop the right attitude toward costs. The same can happen to business organizations. In the end, however, knowing when, how, and which costs to cut requires the right attitude—one that values wise spending, prudent cutting, and organizational flexibility.

The predominant attitude at StarKist to maintain the low-cost producer position created a culture within the company that valued ruthless cost cutting. StarKist, it seemed, would do whatever it took to maintain its low-cost position. No costs were sacred.

Recently, StarKist cut its work force by 5 percent in two tuna-canning factories, one in Puerto Rico and one in American Samoa.

It did so to combat the low-cost operators in Thailand who took home lower wages than StarKist workers. While the 5 percent reduction in work force was perfectly consistent with the company's cultural attitude toward costs, it ultimately led to an overworked staff, with weary fish cleaners leaving tons of meat on the bone every day. In addition to cutting the work force, StarKist had also sped up the production line, forcing the workers to go even faster though no one was paying attention to the amount of meat being left on discarded fish carcasses. It was a classic case of "cutting fat but nicking muscle and bone."

ᘒ The Key Question

How do you develop the right attitude toward costs?

StarKist's Answer

To StarKist's credit, it didn't take too long for someone to recognize that a lot of good tuna was going into the garbage. This realization led to an honest examination of the effects of the work force reduction and the speeding up of the production line, and this analysis, in turn, led to the inescapable conclusion that StarKist's overriding attitude toward cost cutting had actually incurred more costs. Manifesting a lot of cultural flexibility, StarKist managers took the first step toward adjusting their cost-cutting attitude, immediately hiring more people and slowing down the production line. While such a course would have been unthinkable in the past, it now seemed the only viable option. As StarKist refocused its attitude toward cost reduction, it hired 400 extra hourly workers and rehired 15 supervisors and installed 4 more slower processing lines. This action decreased the excessive load on the other lines, and while it was expensive, costing StarKist $5 million in increased labor costs, it also saved $15 million in wastage, a net benefit of $10 million.

Suggested Right Answers

As you evaluate your own cost-cutting attitude and culture, consider the following:

1. *Avoid excessive or overzealous cost-cutting attitudes that can become destructive.*

2. *Be flexible, adopting one attitude during crisis, another during stability.*

3. *Always place cost-cutting attitudes within the context of other strategic, cultural, change, effectiveness, and results issues.*

4. *Move quickly to repair any damage caused by cutting too close to the bone.*

Applying Right Answers

A large industrial manufacturing firm had been cutting costs over the last several years as a means of remaining competitive with foreign producers. According to the Human Resources vice president (I'll call her Susan) the organization's culture had become so aligned with cutting costs that recruitment had suffered. When she researched the problem, she found even more alarming effects. Morale of those already on board had sunk so low, turnover in some key areas of the organization had reached record levels. Could the company's cost-cutting attitude be modified she wondered? To answer that question, she developed a presentation for the chairman and president of the company in which she recommended that the company's tough-minded cost-cutting orientation be replaced with a more "creative-minded" one. The latter approach, she felt, would encourage managers throughout the organization to walk through a creative problem-solving process before automatically opting for a cut in a given area. This process could ensure that people considered a wider range of possibilities and solutions before actually taking action. Wisely, Susan did not want to remove the company's hard-won attitude toward cutting costs but add creative thinking to it.

Agreeing that the new creative approach to problem solving just might work, the chairman and president gave Susan the green light to proceed with her idea on a test basis in one key area of the organization. Within the first year, the new approach to cost cutting was bearing such remarkable fruit, the president approved it for all departments. A cultural change got under way. Now, instead of "Cut at all costs!" people say, "Think before you cut!"

48

Do You Practice the New Art of Cost Cutting?

— ❧ —

*R*ecently, I became quite fond of a young graduate student who was helping me with some research on a book. Married, with a small baby and with almost no financial support from parents, he shouldered most of the burden for his education. He and his young family lived in a modest apartment with none of the luxuries of life, except one. They owned a sophisticated stereo sound system for which they regularly purchased expensive CDs. This seemed in stark contrast with all their other budget constraints. Unable to resist, I asked him about it. He explained that he and his wife loved music, that it brought a peace and calm into their small apartment, reducing their need for other outside entertainment and making the rigors of graduate school tolerable. His words rang true for me because I'd been doing a lot of thinking lately about how the art of cost cutting was changing.

Oil and gas producer, Oryx Energy, has been doing some of the same thinking, too. As the price of a barrel of oil plummeted during the mid-1980s, Oryx cut a lot of people in order to stay alive. But even after cutting loose all the staff it could possibly cut, it still found costs running too high. At this point, Oryx, wondering about alternatives to old-fashioned cost-cutting measures, hired the consulting firm United Research to conduct a comprehensive survey of employees in an effort to discover how they really spent their time. The research uncovered the insight that many employees felt overworked, overly pressured to meet budget targets, and too preoccupied with organizational processes, rules, procedures, reviews, reports, and approvals. Consequently, they spent only a fraction of their time discovering and producing more oil.

With help from United Research, Oryx executives developed teams throughout the organization to look at what work the company could and should eliminate. These teams made countless recommendations, which ultimately led to a 25 percent reduction of internal reporting requirements, a scaling down of the number of approvals required for capital expenditures, and a collapse of the time it took to prepare the annual budget from seven months to six weeks. In the process, the firm eliminated many middle-management jobs because that work no longer existed. Oryx had discovered the new art of cost cutting by eliminating *unnecessary work*.

❧ The Key Question

How do you learn the new art of cost cutting?

Oryx Energy's Answer

The new art of cost cutting depends on identifying work that does not accomplish the basic strategic objectives of the business. According to Oryx, to cut costs wisely, you first ask people in the organization to identify the work that does not help them perform the strategic tasks necessary to make money in the business. As a result, Oryx discovered an enormous amount of wasted or needless work. Through its work-elimination program, Oryx liberated the power of its employees to pursue new drilling technology, make new discoveries, and obtain new reserves. Oryx, now the largest independent oil and gas producer in the world, has cut the cost of finding new oil and gas in half, and it is effectively replacing the reserves it depletes through production. Oryx saved an estimated $70 million in operating costs in 1990 and has positioned itself well for the post-Gulf War era.

Suggested Right Answers

The new art of cost cutting requires that you:

1. *Cut out all unnecessary work.*

2. *Eliminate all unnecessary rules, procedures, processes, reports, reviews, and activities that are not vital to your business.*

3. *Put quality and customer satisfaction first, and never cut activities necessary to deliver quality and satisfaction.*

4. *Continually review all work with an eye to cutting whatever doesn't get results.*

5. *Never start your cost-cutting efforts with people.*

6. *Communicate constantly and clearly with everyone in your organization regarding exactly what you expect in terms of cost cutting.*

7. *Avoid overworking or overburdening your people.*

Applying Right Answers

Facing a number of changes in the economy and industry, an aircraft manufacturer recently went through a cost-cutting frenzy and laid off a great number of people. When the layoffs hit, two associates at the company (I'll call them Cheryl and Judy) each had something different happen to them—Cheryl got a pink slip, while Judy kept her job. Since they were close friends, they continued their relationship even after the layoffs. Cheryl, who enjoyed her job and was reluctant to move from the area, took a temporary position with a local engineering firm in the hopes that the company would rehire her in a few months. During this miserable period of her life, time seemed to drag on, and she began to resent the company. Why had she been laid off? Hadn't she been contributing?

Meanwhile, was Judy happy? Surprisingly, no. While she had retained her job, life in the company became increasingly unbearable as she found herself pressured to work 70 hours a week just to keep up with burdensome schedules. Unable to spend time with her husband and small child, she felt herself burning out on the job. Consequently, she, too, came to resent the company. When Cheryl and Judy met for dinner one evening, they were surprised at how miserable each other felt. Judy had thought Cheryl would be happy for not having to deal with the company's work environment, while Cheryl had thought Judy would be delighted over keeping her job. They both decided to turn their backs on the company and move their careers in other directions.

As many other people fled the environment, company management came to realize that it had cut too deeply and that it should pursue other measures to reduce costs. Within a year, the company tried to rehire 35 percent of the people it had laid off, but many, like Cheryl and Judy, didn't trust the organization anymore. It turned out that by cutting people, instead of work, during times of change, the company had cut the wrong costs and lost the commitment and support of their people. Such costs can be the costliest expense any organization can incur.

49

What Can You Yourself Do to Cut Costs?

In his book *Save the Earth at Work*, environmentalist Steve Bennett points out that American businesses discard about 25 million pounds of printer and typewriter ribbons annually. The U.S. Postal Service alone spends $5 million per year on replacement ribbons. Yet few people realize that a typical ribbon can be re-inked 100 times before it needs to be thrown out. At one Boston law firm, one secretary who learned how to re-ink typewriter ribbons convinced the partners of the firm to let her institute a program for reducing office waste. In one year, her efforts saved over 180 ribbons at an average of $7 each. Imagine 1000 companies following that one secretary's lead. Not only would the savings total over $1 million, the environment would benefit from a ton of less waste. One person really can make a big difference!

Hughes Aircraft, part of GM Hughes Electronics, operates in a tough business where costs must be carefully monitored. Like many companies, Hughes has implemented a cost-improvement program designed to involve individuals in cost-reduction efforts. The best way to cut costs, Hughes feels, is to get people to start thinking differently and acting more responsibly. To implement that approach, Hughes Aircraft's cost-improvement program involves and recognizes individual employees for their contributions. Everyone, including line workers, supervisors, and managers, in all departments and divisions of the company from engineering to manufacturing, are invited to submit cost-cutting suggestions. Operating on the assumption that workers themselves know the most about their own specific jobs, the company allows every person to act as an expert in his or her own work area.

This philosophy has made Hughes Aircraft employees more accountable for cost improvements. They find cost-improvement suggestion forms available throughout company facilities. Once their suggestions are filed, management and improvement committees review them carefully. When a suggestion is approved, the company specifically recognizes the achievement through commendations and rewards. In this way, Hughes tells its people: Each individual can make a big difference.

ᨠ The Key Question

How do you empower individual people to think in terms of cost containment?

Hughes Aircraft's Answer

Not only does Hughes make individuals responsible for suggestions, it allows them the authority to implement them. In one instance, a team of workers who build satellites made certain suggestions for cost improvements that they ultimately received encouragement to implement. Working together, employees in design, manufacturing, purchasing, and marketing found 131 steps in the construction process of satellites they felt could be tightened. Eventually limiting their efforts to the 30 most urgent steps, the ones with the highest probable payoff, they took swift action making modifications in the construction process that ended up slashing the time for building a satellite control processor from 45 weeks to 22 weeks. This single cost-improvement effort saved the company millions of dollars.

Suggested Right Answers

To place responsibility for cost-improvement programs in the hands of individual people:

1. *Recognize individuals as experts in their jobs.*

2. *Ask people individually to help improve costs.*

3. *Carefully review every single suggestion your people make about cost improvement.*

4. *Keep individuals who have offered suggestions informed of the status of those suggestions.*

5. *Afford individuals and teams of individuals the responsibility to act upon suggestions.*

6. *Recognize and reward the people who make suggestions that end up saving money.*

7. *Publicize the positive results of actions taken by people and teams to improve costs.*

8. *Pass some of the cost savings on to your employees in one way or another, in the form of bonuses, opportunities, additional resources, increased budgets, or other personally motivating and stimulating rewards.*

Applying Right Answers

Gain-sharing or cost-improvement-sharing has been around for a long time as a concept, and many organizations have tried to implement it. However, it's often difficult to separate out the respective contributions associated with a given suggestion, i.e., making it, fleshing it out, developing it, and mobilizing to implement it. If the process of identifying who deserves credit bogs down, a suggestion program can fail to empower people.

A project manager and design engineer for a large electronics company (I'll call him Chuck) had won a reputation as a real leader of the company's cost-improvement programs. While the company had experimented with sharing the benefits of cost-improvement savings with employees, the process kept getting gummed up.

Since Chuck had successfully completed three projects that achieved remarkable cost improvements, he felt he had gained an understanding of how the process should work. Just as the company was on the verge of abandoning its latest benefit-sharing program, Chuck asked his boss to let him experiment with a new plan he was convinced would work. His plan was simple. Whenever a particular suggestion for cost improvement in a department or on a project received approval, every individual who contributed or wanted to contribute in any way to the effort would be drawn into what Chuck called a "pool of contributors." This pool would be responsible for making a cost-improvement suggestion a reality. Not only would the team call its own shots about how to proceed, it would also determine benefit sharing within general parameters set by senior management.

When Chuck's boss criticized the plan as overly idealistic, claiming that counterproductive squabbles would arise within the contributor pool, Chuck defended his plan by saying, "We must think of our cost-improvement projects as mini-organizations within the company. They can take on a life of their own, with members feeling a sense of involvement and responsibility. I've seen it happen. A strong bond builds among contributing team members by the time you get through, and never once have I seen the originators of an idea claim more credit than they deserve, nor fail to appreciate those who sweated blood to make it a reality."

In the end, Chuck convinced his boss to let him try it. When he put the new plan into effect on his next cost-improvement suggestion, it worked like a charm. Percentages of the cost-improvement benefits went to 15 different members of the contributor pool as an immediate cash bonus. Every member of the team loved the process and welcomed the tangible reward, especially Chuck, who watched as his plan was adopted company-wide, ushering in a whole new era of personalizing the need for cost improvements.

50

Are Your Profits Cost Effective?

ٱ

Over the years, I have done quite a bit of work for snack food companies, so I pay attention to new products that show up on the shelves and usually try those that catch my eye. When I saw a new muffin snack pack recently, I tried the product and enjoyed it a lot. As usually happens, I bought the product for a few weeks and then moved on to something else. Several months later, I tried the muffins again and was shocked to find they were a lot smaller than before. Of course, I felt cheated. Sure, the company was probably making more money on the smaller-size product, but not from me. In this case, cutting costs to increase profits may not have been cost effective for the company in the long run.

Like all of the other Bell operating companies, U.S. West found itself heavily overstaffed when it came into being several years ago. There were just too many people doing too many things that didn't need to be done. Consequently, since 1984, the company has been trying to downsize, cutting several thousand employees in an effort to reduce costs and improve profits. Still, it needed more. U.S. West employees may have been getting more efficient, but were they getting more effective? No one seemed to know the answer until Gary Ames, CEO of a subsidiary of the regional

Bell operating company, took the bull by the horns. Even though several thousand people had been cut from the payroll and profits were up, Ames believed that productivity at U.S. West was still unacceptably low and performance was less than winning. In winning. In short, he felt the company had not yet achieved cost-effective profits.

❧ The Key Question

How do you make sure that your costs deliver the maximum profit in the long term?

U.S. West's Answer

To solve the problem, Ames went through a process of identifying what the subsidiary was really trying to accomplish in terms of bottom-line results, both tangible and intangible. Through that process, he pinpointed a number of activities and agendas that to his mind didn't seem cost effective. However, he resisted making personnel cuts because he did not feel certain that doing so would increase cost effectiveness or long-term growth and profitability. Sure, such cuts would improve cost efficiency, but would they really improve the company's ability to obtain certain strategically important results.

At that point, Ames assigned 17 senior executives to a special task force charged for three months with examining 7000 middle managers to determine how they spent their time on an hourly basis each and every day. Basically, Ames wanted to find out, once and for all, whether the money that the company was spending on payroll and other expenses was being effectively spent. It didn't surprise him when the task force found that many activities and tasks being performed by these 7000 middle managers had little or nothing to do with achieving the strategic results desired by U.S. West.

In one case, 350 people were involved in developing the subsidiary's annual budget. Ames felt that number should be less than 100. And that was just one of several such examples of ineffective expenditures throughout the subsidiary. For Gary Ames, the goal was not a matter of working harder or working cheaper, it was a matter of working with a clearer focus on results. Only then could U.S. West make its people productive and its profits cost effective.

Suggested Right Answers

As you attempt to make your own organization's profits more cost effective:

1. *Don't waste time and talent on nonproductive or nonstrategic, tasks and activities.*

2. *Don't waste careers by allowing people to think they are doing something meaningful and results oriented when they are not.*

3. *Don't waste energy trying to work harder or smarter, but work with more clarity regarding results.*

4. *Don't waste money on anything that does not help you meet strategic objectives.*

5. *Don't waste emotions by making people wait and wonder when the ax is going to fall.*

6. *Don't waste words by beating around the bush, but make everyone conscious of the organization's cost-effectiveness goals.*

7. *Don't waste priorities on anything that doesn't get you where you want your organization to go.*

8. *Don't waste opportunities to cut ineffective costs.*

Applying Right Answers

A turnaround specialist (I'll call him Lee) was brought in to help a conglomerate sitting on the edge of bankruptcy. Lee didn't have much time, so he worked quickly to liquidate assets that could provide the cash flow necessary for keeping the business afloat. After effecting major personnel cuts in several divisions, he began to sell off some of the other divisions to correct the downslide and the losses that had been accumulating for the past several years. Initially, it appeared that Lee had really achieved a turnaround with the company, as the conglomerate reported profits for the first time in six years. However, since the profits were born out of the liquidation of assets and the cutting of personnel, sales eventually declined. Still, the board of directors was so happy with the unexpected profit that they ignored the long-term impact of what was happening to the company.

Over the next two years, it became apparent that the conglomerate had developed problems much deeper than anyone supposed. The remaining divisions were just not able to function effectively in terms of generating revenues or producing profits. Lee, again looking for cuts that would shore up the financial picture, sold additional assets and laid off more people. For four straight years, the company showed profits but on an annually decreasing sales base. Finally, the surviving divisions were so damaged by the personnel cuts that the businesses had to be sold before they became worthless. Lee had no choice but to liquidate the entire operation.

Eventually, all of the businesses within the conglomerate were sold or closed. Bad debts were written off, and the conglomerate went quietly out of business. There had never really been a turnaround; costs had merely been cut and assets liquidated in order to reduce debt and maintain the payment of dividends to shareholders. In the end, the conglomerate's profits over those few years of the supposed turnaround had become cost destructive. In other words, it won profits by cutting the very costs that could sustain profits in the future.

Afterword

———————— ❧ ————————

Genius not only diagnoses the situation but
supplies the right answer.

Robert Graves

Over the past decade, business-people have been inundated with theories about why enterprises succeed or fail. We've heard about strategic vision, cultural values, corporate renewal, and learning organizations. We've been urged to create high-quality products, totally satisfied customers, and deeply committed employees. And we've striven mightily to understand and apply a bewildering number of trendy ideas, from cross-functional knowledge teams to one-on-one marketing to cluster organizations.

Every one of these theories contains a kernel of truth, but in the hectic day-to-day turmoil where we do our work, whether it's a home-based consulting office or the executive suite of a global enterprise, the urgency of immediate concerns tends to prevent us from pausing, stepping back, and asking (not to mention answering) all the crucial questions that will determine the ultimate outcome of our endeavors. As we tend to this week's paramount problem or next week's anticipated crisis, we invariably lose sight of the larger context in which our businesses operate.

It's time, I think, for every manager and executive to adopt a perspective with which he or she can ponder tough, vital questions, conducting a series of rigorous experiments that test every major performance variable. Just as a chemist uses a litmus test to determine the quality of a substance, you can apply a crucial acid test to every single aspect of your organization by asking and answering all of the right questions.

The Acid Test grid that concludes this book matches today's 10 major business issues with 5 key performance areas. It provides a handy way of getting a "satellite's view" of your organization. But to gain maximum benefits from your mental exercises, I suggest you answer the questions for yourself and your team as well as for your organization. For example, you may answer Question 9 the same for yourself and for your team but differently for your organization. After further discussion or analysis of the question, you might alter your perception of your own, your team's, or your organization's performance in that area. Ultimately, of course, you will try to make some specific and practical decisions about strengthening weaknesses or further bolstering strengths.

Make copies of the Acid Test grid, if you'd like, to use in your organization. As with the rest of the book, you can conduct your assessments before reading any or all of the book, after you've completed any part of it, or as concluding wrap-up after you've worked your way through all the questions.

Once you have assessed yourself, your team, and your organization, you should have developed a pretty clear picture of what might be done to make yourself and your organization stronger. Whether you end up deciding to pursue the Malcolm Baldridge Award, create a new strategic business unit, embark on a cost-cutting program, develop a stronger business plan, increase employee commitment, adopt a new channel of distribution, enhance team effectiveness, or just boost bottom-line results, this exercise should set you on a path toward finding the right answers to tough questions.

PERFORMANCE AREAS

BUSINESS ISSUES	STRATEGY	CULTURE	CHANGE	EFFECTIVENESS	RESULTS
Customers	*Question 1* What customer needs are you trying to satisfy?	*Question 2* Do you make customer satisfaction a total concern?	*Question 3* Do you carefully track changing customer needs?	*Question 4* Is your job tied to customer satisfaction?	*Question 5* Can you consistently get and keep customers?
Quality	*Question 6* What level of quality are you really after?	*Question 7* Are you delivering the quality you promise?	*Question 8* Do you continuously improve quality?	*Question 9* Can you get each individual to improve quality?	*Question 10* Do you always deliver above-standard products or services?
Service	*Question 11* Do you segment markets by service expectation?	*Question 12* Are you providing the service customers want?	*Question 13* Should you change the type or level of service you provide?	*Question 14* Who assumes responsibility for service?	*Question 15* What does service really do for you?
Advantage	*Question 16* Do you fully exploit competitive advantages?	*Question 17* Do your advantages match your values?	*Question 18* Can you sustain your advantages?	*Question 19* Does everyone work to sustain your advantages?	*Question 20* Are your advantages paying off?
Talent	*Question 21* Do you recognize your own genius?	*Question 22* Do you fully appreciate everyone's talents?	*Question 23* Can you find new ways to apply existing talents?	*Question 24* Are you maximizing talents?	*Question 25* Do you have the right talents to succeed?

Motivation	*Question 26* What strategic priorities motivate you most?	*Question 27* What values do people hold widely and feel deeply?	*Question 28* Do you resist or relish change?	*Question 29* Who's motivated and who's not?	*Question 30* Does your motivation get results?
Trust	*Question 31* Do you maintain clear strategic vision?	*Question 32* Are you trustworthy?	*Question 33* Do you keep the borders to change open?	*Question 34* Do you strive for consistency and reliability?	*Question 35* Does trust produce results?
Technology	*Question 36* Do you apply strategically appropriate technology?	*Question 37* Does your culture embrace new technology?	*Question 38* Are you behind or ahead of the technology wave?	*Question 39* Does technology empower you?	*Question 40* Can you evaluate the worth of your technology edge?
Alliances	*Question 41* Do you know how to locate new allies?	*Question 42* Do you form long- or short-term alliances?	*Question 43* When should you change alliances?	*Question 44* Do your alliances make sense to everyone involved?	*Question 45* Have alliances increased your competitiveness?
Costs	*Question 46* Can you define your strategic costs?	*Question 47* What's your attitude toward costs?	*Question 48* Do you practice the new art of cost cutting?	*Question 49* What can you yourself do to cut costs?	*Question 50* Are your profits cost effective?

Index